To Bridget & Ian

with affection & in friendship,

Anthony .

The Water's Edge

With love to Asnat

Maia, Shirin and Koram

The Water's Edge

Meetings of image and word

Ardyn Halter

poems by

Jennie Feldman, Seamus Heaney, Geoffrey Hill, Gabriel Levin
Michael Longley, Jamie McKendrick, Paul Muldoon
Don Paterson, Robin Robertson, Stephen Romer

Published in 2006 by

Lund Humphries
Gower House
Croft Road
Aldershot
Hampshire GU11 3HR

and

Lund Humphries
Suite 420
101 Cherry Street
Burlington
VT 05401-4405
USA

www.lundhumphries.com
Lund Humphries is part of Ashgate Publishing

British Library Cataloguing-in-Publication Data
A catalogue record for this book is available from the British Library

ISBN
0 85331 950 2
978-0-85331-950-4

Library of Congress number 2006927558

Designed by Ardyn Halter and Sally Jeffery
Printed in Italy by Graphicom

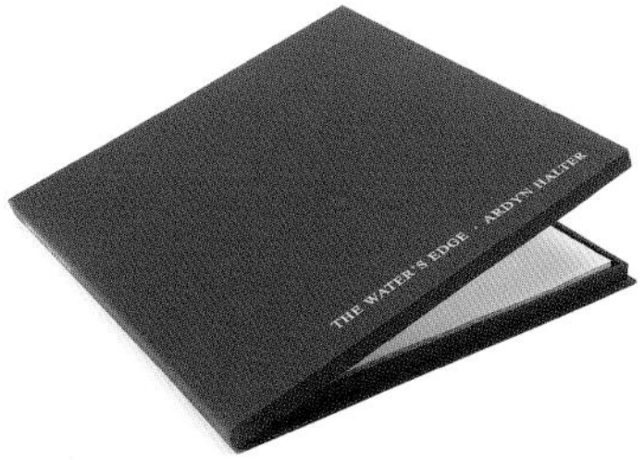
THE WATER'S EDGE · ARDYN HALTER

Part One

Prints and Poems

Gulf
detail
(see p. 11)

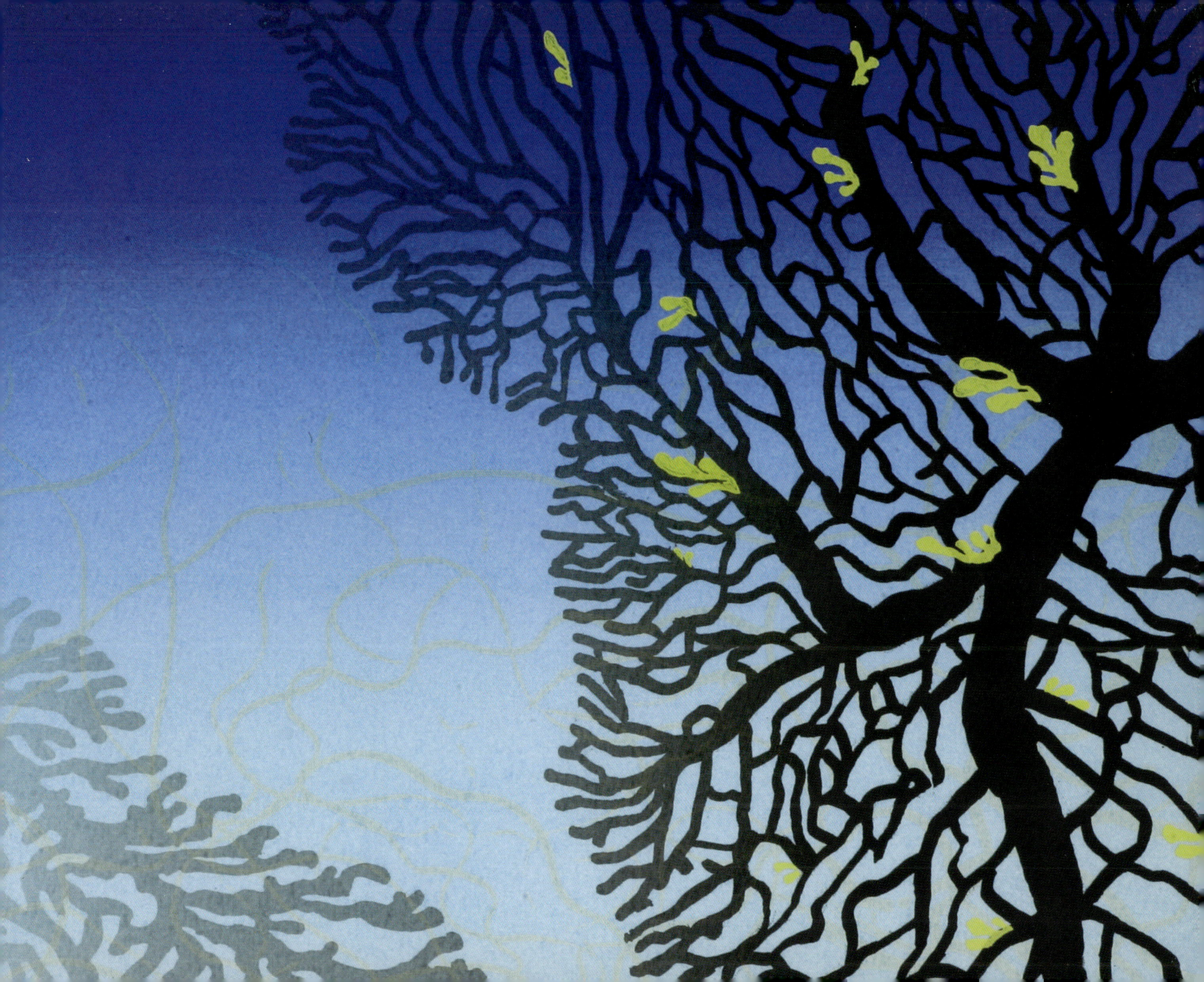

A Note

These prints, which form the series *The Water's Edge*, are not illustrations of poems. The poems, with one exception, were written before the prints were made and do not relate directly to visual art. They are presented here in tandem. Common to them all is the sense of water as a primary element in the emotional or psychological consciousness of the writer. In Stephen Romer's poem *Coming Back*, the entire poem reads like an incoming tide, a single sentence, a flow with its own subtle internal currents which eventually leads the reader to sand, to shore. In Seamus Heaney's poem *Limbo*, water is the medium of death, a limbo tract, neutral and numbing in its cold, just as the woman's deed has emotionally numbed her. To Don Paterson, in *Shhh*, the sea is an echo in his inner ear, confused amongst sounds and experiences, amplified physically within him. And Paterson's sonnet shares with Gabriel Levin's sonnet *Mediterranean* the intensity of the experience of the sound of waves: '. . . the surf's short-breathed plosives detonating in their ears.'

Paul Muldoon's sonnet *The Merman* is about the meeting point of sea and land, the death of a man at sea and in a conversational, dialectic manner, the shore becomes a meeting point, reflecting shore into sea, sea

Gulf
Hand-printed silkscreen print
image: 30.5 × 30.5 cm; 12 × 12 in
paper: 52.5 × 50 cm; 21.5 × 21.5 in

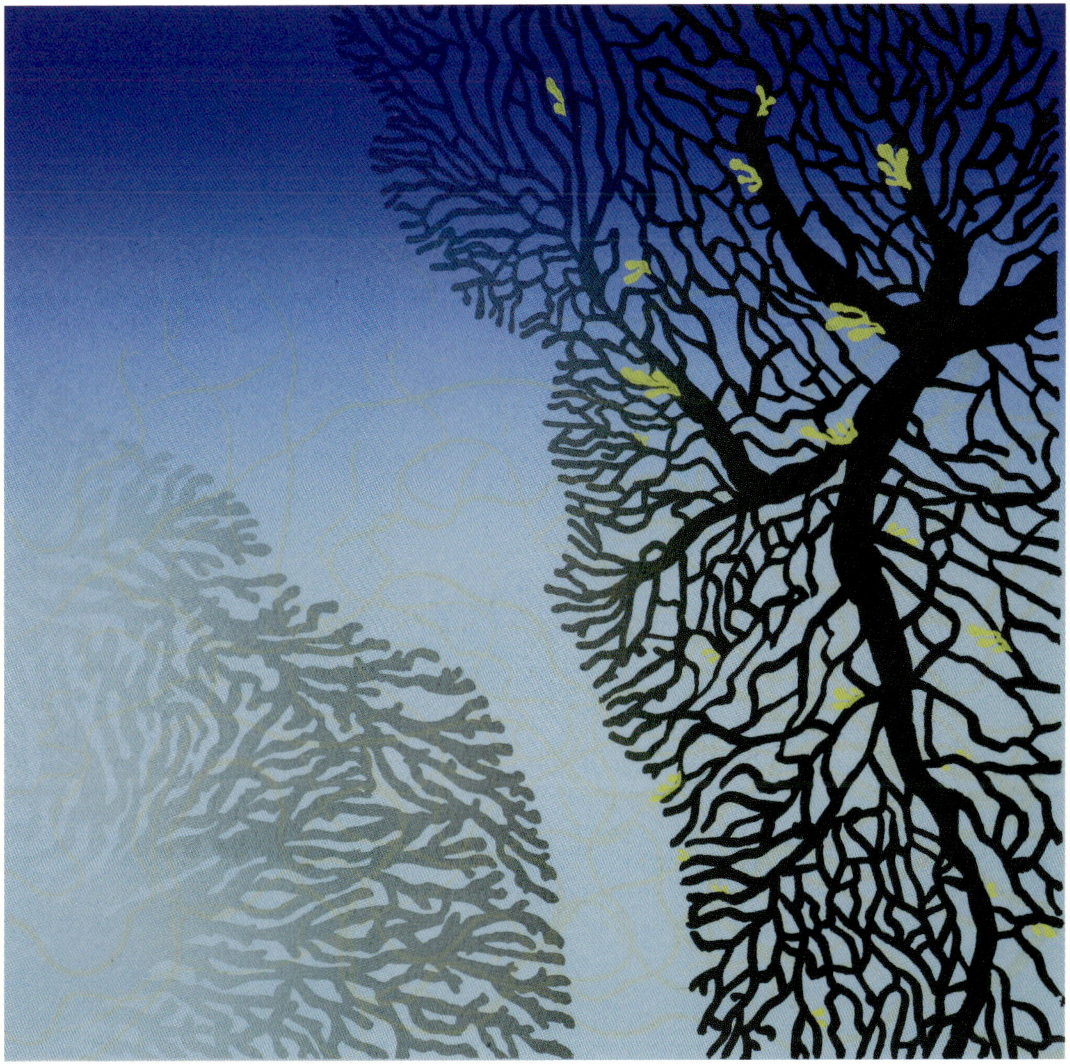

into shore. So, by the end of the poem, 'the cries of one in difficulties' could be one at sea or on shore, so fully has the poem consummated the interchange of the two elements.

Jamie McKendrick's *Margin* is firmly positioned on shore, looking along the shoreline at human activity. In common with Geoffrey Hill's *The White Ship* McKendrick alludes to mythology, but whereas McKendrick's poem leads back to mythology, Geoffrey Hill sees 'seaman / And king's son also' pass '. . . through the wet sieve / Without enrichment or decay' – mythology and contemporary, highborn and commoner commingled.

In Michael Longley's *Water-burn* and *The Comber* water and sea are quintessential, kinetic, vital. In his wonderfully charged poems and the other poems selected here it is apparent that when we think about, view, reflect on, relate to the sea and living water, we are affected in a primary way. It touches on deep emotions, like one's earliest memories. The shades of grey, blue, green and white we see when we look at water, the delicacies and subtleties of colour are somehow transposed into simple, strong, primary emotions. So in these prints I wanted to reverse that process. I sought to express the colours of our, or at least my sensory and emotional reactions to water, to the sea – to being in it, beside it, with it. Those primal and primary responses to water and sea are carried in our innermost ear like the furled core of a conch. With few exceptions they suggest to me a primary palette.

I have not sought to illustrate the poems. To do so would be to belittle them, to impose upon them or to confine their scope. And it seemed necessary to resist the easy path of giving a single image to each poem. Seeing the one would affect the way one might view the other – like a book cover design influencing one's attitude towards a book each time one picks it up.

Rather than this, it is my hope that seeing the one might affect one's eyes, might change one's attitude to the other, just as reading the poem could subsequently affect the way in which our eyes see colour. At the very least, it might slow down the way we view. Conversely, the images might alter one's tempo of reading. The order of the viewing and the reading does not matter. There is no sequence. Only I feel they should not follow a regimented pattern of poem, print, poem, print.

One last point: why sonnets and short poems? Well, as Don Paterson has said, the sonnet's fourteen lines forms almost a square of text on the page. It looks self-contained. And I sought poems our eyes meet with a single look, do not overflow the page, images contained in themselves.

Ardyn Halter

Water-burn

We should have been galloping on horses, their hoofprints
Splashes of light, divots kicked out of the darkness,
Or hauling up lobster pots in a wake of sparks. Where
Were the otters and seals? Were the dolphins on fire?
Yes, we should have been doing more with our lives.

Michael Longley

From *The Weather in Japan*, Jonathan Cape, 2000

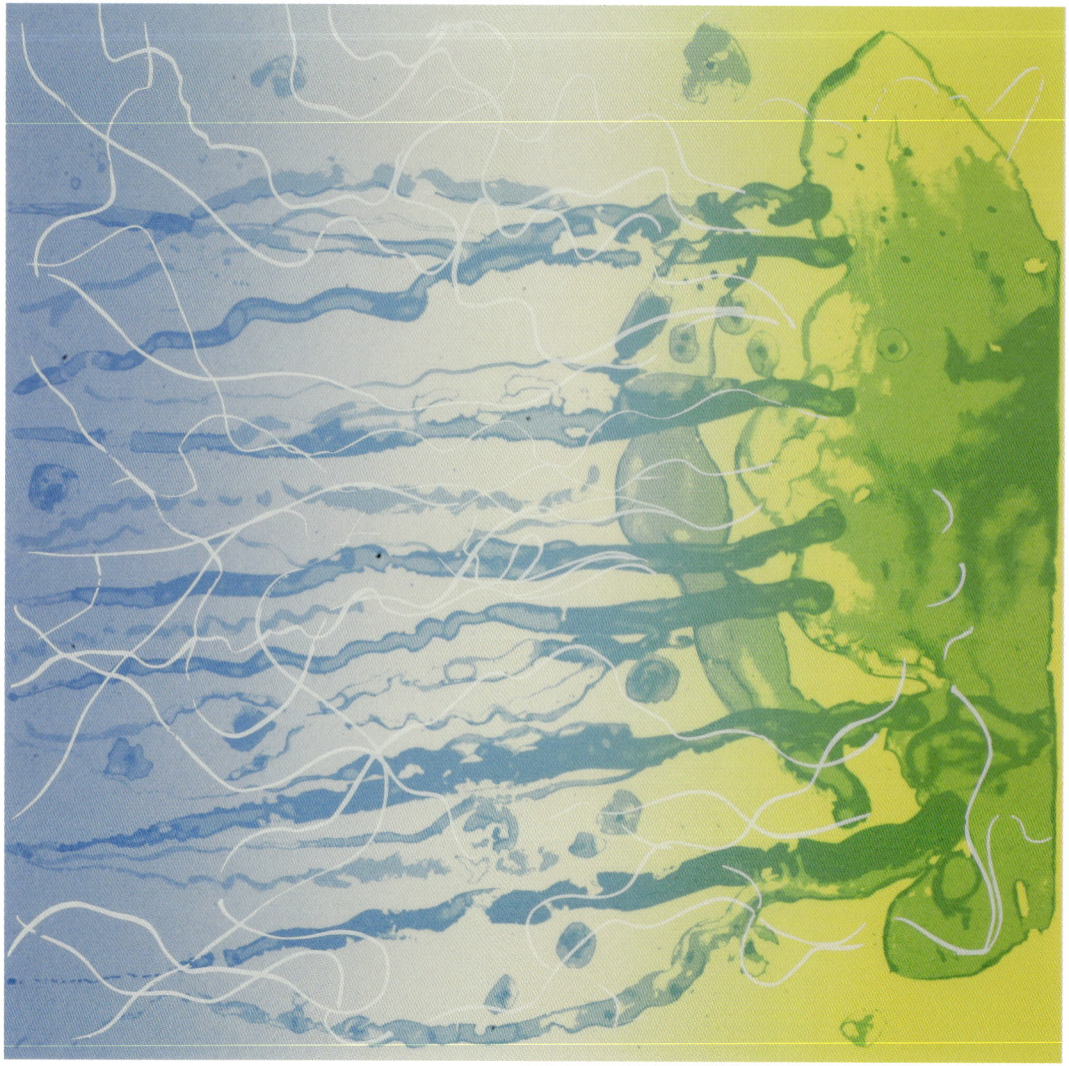

Medusa
Hand-printed silkscreen print
image size: 30.5 × 30.5 cm, 12 × 12 in
paper size: 52.5 × 50 cm, 21.5 × 19.5 in

Mediterranean

Murex shells – the royal dye long squeezed
out of the hypobronchial gland – litter
the shore, where Sea People once heaved
long ships into the eastern basin, seeking her
who'd given them the slip: *Beauty*
they hallooed in her wake, or some such name
barked from the belly at the crass mutiny.
In their polychrome robes they stood in vain
gaping at the sea, the surf's short-
breathed plosives detonating in their ears.
Now I skin the busy beach for sport,
Lady-of-the-Sea, forever in arrears
of love, ears cocked to the pulmonary beat
of young hearts primed by the heat.

Gabriel Levin

Are Coral Made
Hand-printed silkscreen print
image size: 30.5 × 30.5 cm; 12 × 12 in
paper size: 52.5 × 50 cm; 21.5 × 19.5 in

From *Sleepers of Beulah*, Sinclair-Stevenson, 1992

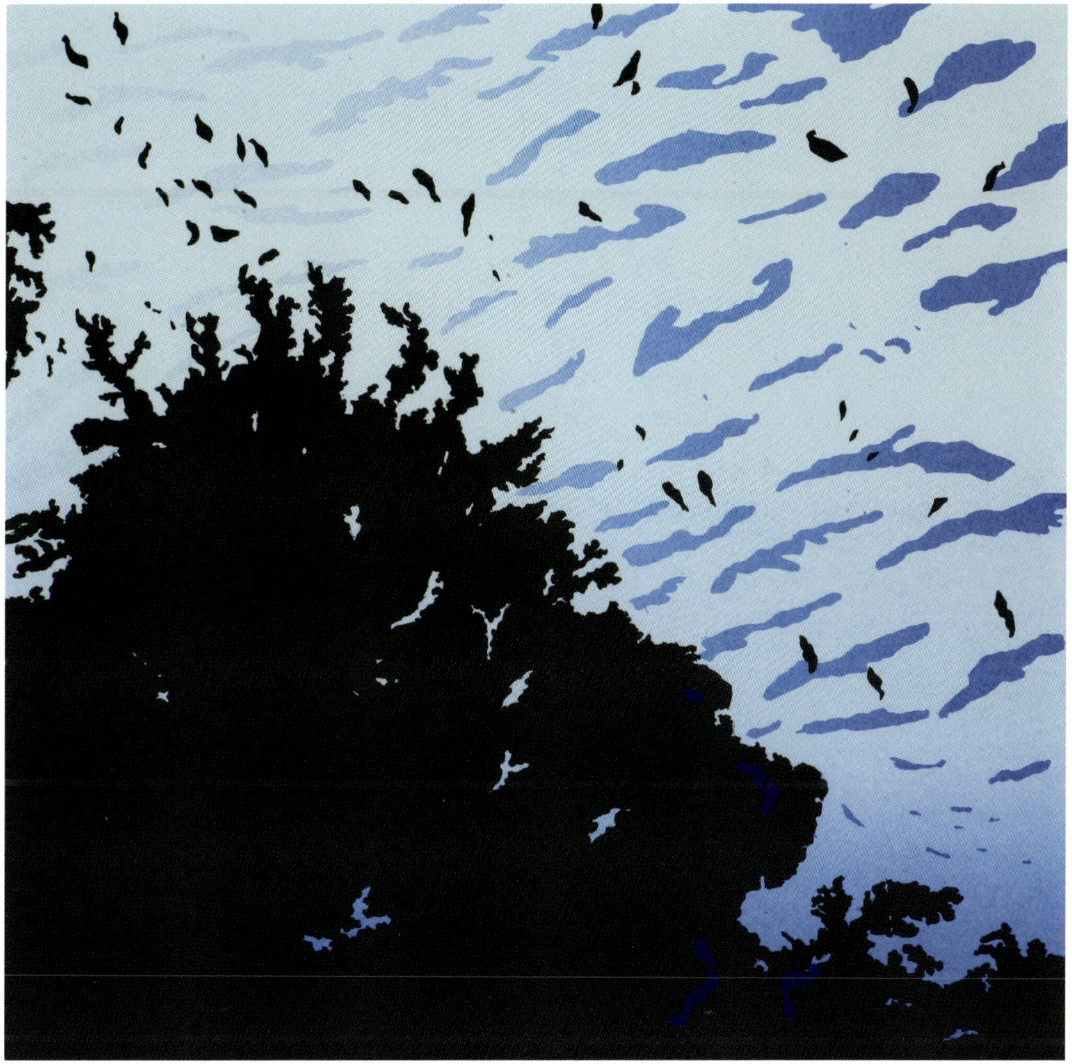

Sea Change

From the ancient shores of Caesarea just west of his home Ardyn Halter gently pulls us under the blue hood of the Mediterranean. His perspective is unique, as he paints not the sea's undulant mantle but rather its sub-aquatic realm. Here a strong, confident swimmer might navigate, relying on a good pair of lungs and the sun's rays penetrating and scattering its refracted light below. Halter's sensory vision fins its way through a liquid world of alluring, enigmatic beauty. Though being co-extensive, at least in the life of the imagination, with the human body (*Are Coral Made*) such beauty is finely tinged as well by what Rilke called 'the beginning of terror'. The silkscreen, with its step by step overlaying of tonal values – and one of the pleasures of running one's eyes over print after print is in noting the subtle gradations of blues, from cerulean blue to azure, ultramarine and cobalt – may very well be the perfect medium in which to capture the particular sensation of immersion, of envelopment, as in *Underwavebreak*, *Coming Up For Air*, and *Medusa*, where we are looking, as it were, from the bottom up, with suspended breath.

English-born and living for the last twenty years on 'this eastern strand' of the Mediterranean, Halter's prints attest to an ongoing exchange, an intimate mute commerce, between the painter and his natural surroundings, internalized and, one might say, reduced to its essentials. For the ocean as a living, suspiring organism is a truth that courses through the painter's veins. Halter's prints are consequently not simple visual representations, but rather tactile, haptic apprehensions of what he calls the 'border breath' in which we live. Hence Halter must, paradoxically, disengage himself from the immediate spectacle of the sea (the craft of printing is executed over extended periods in London) in the interest of engendering sea-born images on paper that reveal an unfolding process of loss – erasure, at a technical level – retrieval and re-creation whose final incarnations are of singular grace.

Perhaps they are also in the end – and so the aptly titled *Proteus* would suggest – 'the mimic force of every savage shape', and as such Halter has grappled, albeit on the grounds of the printing surface, with the elusive sea god of ever changing guises, who must be surprised and held down fast before yielding his true form.

Gabriel Levin

Limbo

Fishermen at Ballyshannon
Netted an infant last night
Along with the salmon.
An illegitimate spawning,

A small one thrown back
To the waters. But I'm sure
As she stood in the shallows
Ducking him tenderly

Till the frozen knobs of her wrists
Were dead as the gravel,
He was a minnow with hooks
Tearing her open.

She waded in under
The sign of her cross.
He was hauled in with the fish.
Now limbo will be

A cold glitter of souls
Through some far briny zone.
Even Christ's palms, unhealed,
Smart and cannot fish there.

Seamus Heaney

From *Wintering Out*, Faber and Faber, 1972

Fluke
detail
(see p. 34)

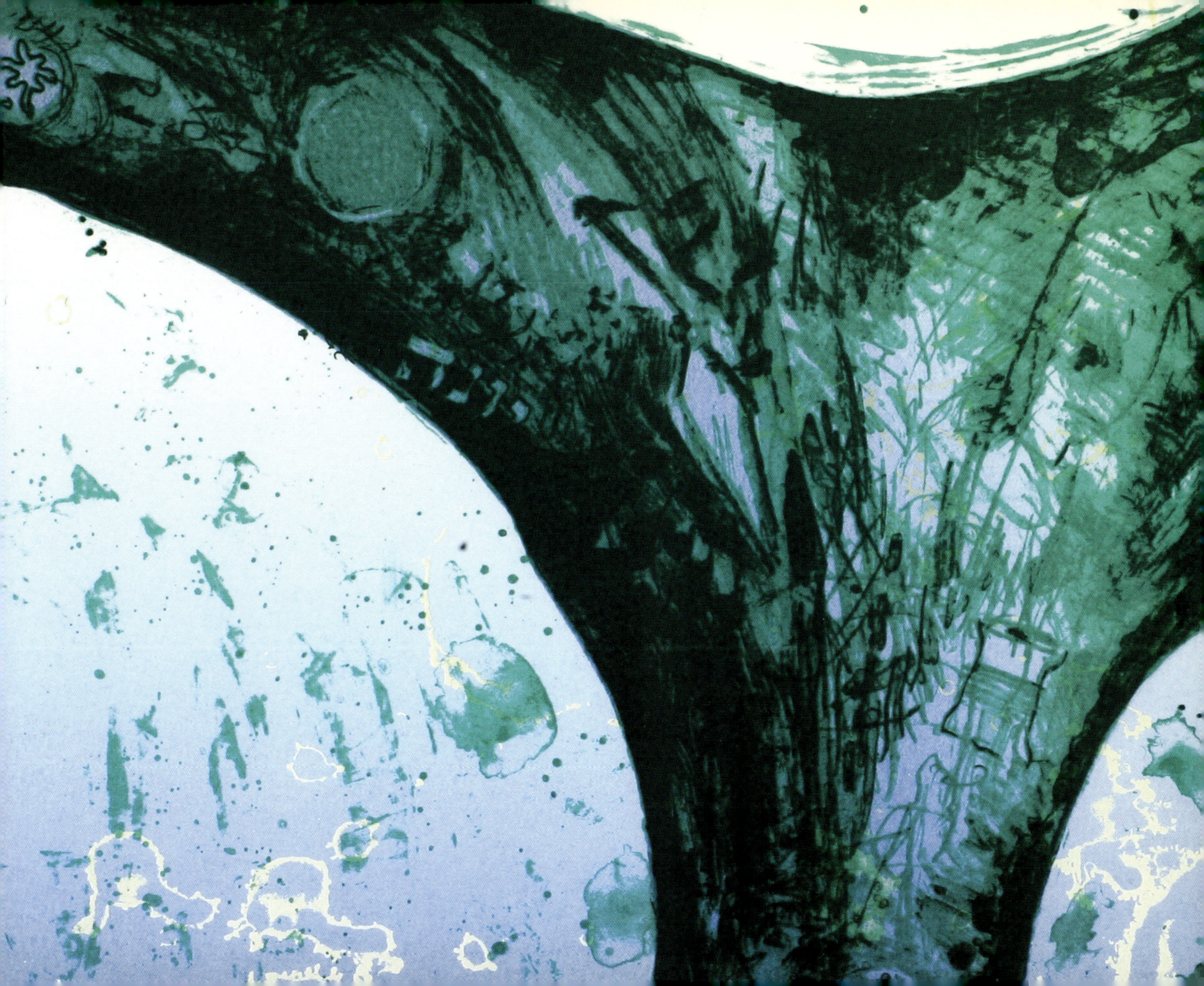

Shoal Passage
Hand-printed silkscreen print
image size: 30.5 × 30.5 cm; 12 × 12 in
paper size: 52.5 × 50 cm; 21.5 × 19.5 in

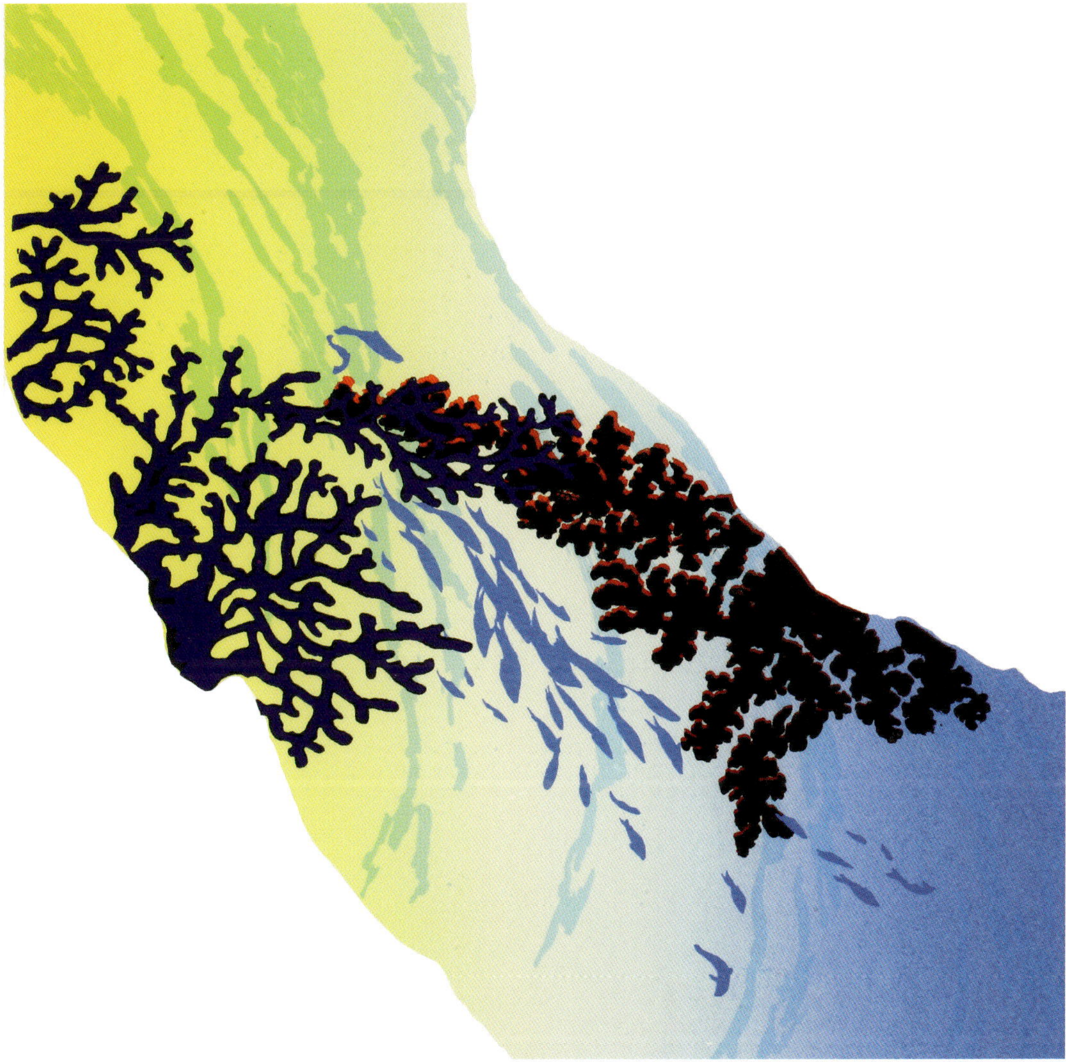

Coming back
(*for James Malpas*)

When the something withdrawn (you cannot tell
exactly what or when) flows back into the blood
and you return from the damned into your own
(where living is at last to be living now
which the damned cannot know); when your beloved
is again beloved, and morning shows a tree
dressed in light, meaning and memory
at peace in its leaves; when your thought is cool
as linen and you go downstairs to receive
a letter from a friend with total recall
who tells you what you were, and you listen
with attention to rain on the skylight
which tells you what you are
                                        then you know
that nothing is lost or gone to waste
that it cannot start again; as when you leave
the city for the pulling air and the sea
which turns upon itself and fills you, something
bows you down to the ground, bows you weeping
down to the sand, weeping there and giving thanks.

Stephen Romer

From *Idols*, Oxford University Press, 1986

Margin

Some played volleyball using fishing nets;
some drank cans of Peroni; others searched
inland for flints and sources of clear water.

I wandered by the shore towards the harbour
and the blind lighthouse of Palinurus,
and found a dolphin turning at the tide's hem

bluntly, its skin fraying on the sharp stones;
then the stringy, knifed wheeze of the helmsman
came back from the shadows and a light struck

fire through the mute larynx of the rock
at Cumae – the mad woman humming just to calm him:
That cruel place will always bear your name.

Jamie McKendrick

From *The Sirocco Room*, Faber and Faber, 1991

Red Sea
Hand-printed silkscreen print
image size: 30.5 × 30.5 cm; 12 × 12 in
paper size 52.5 × 50 cm; 21.5 × 19.5 in

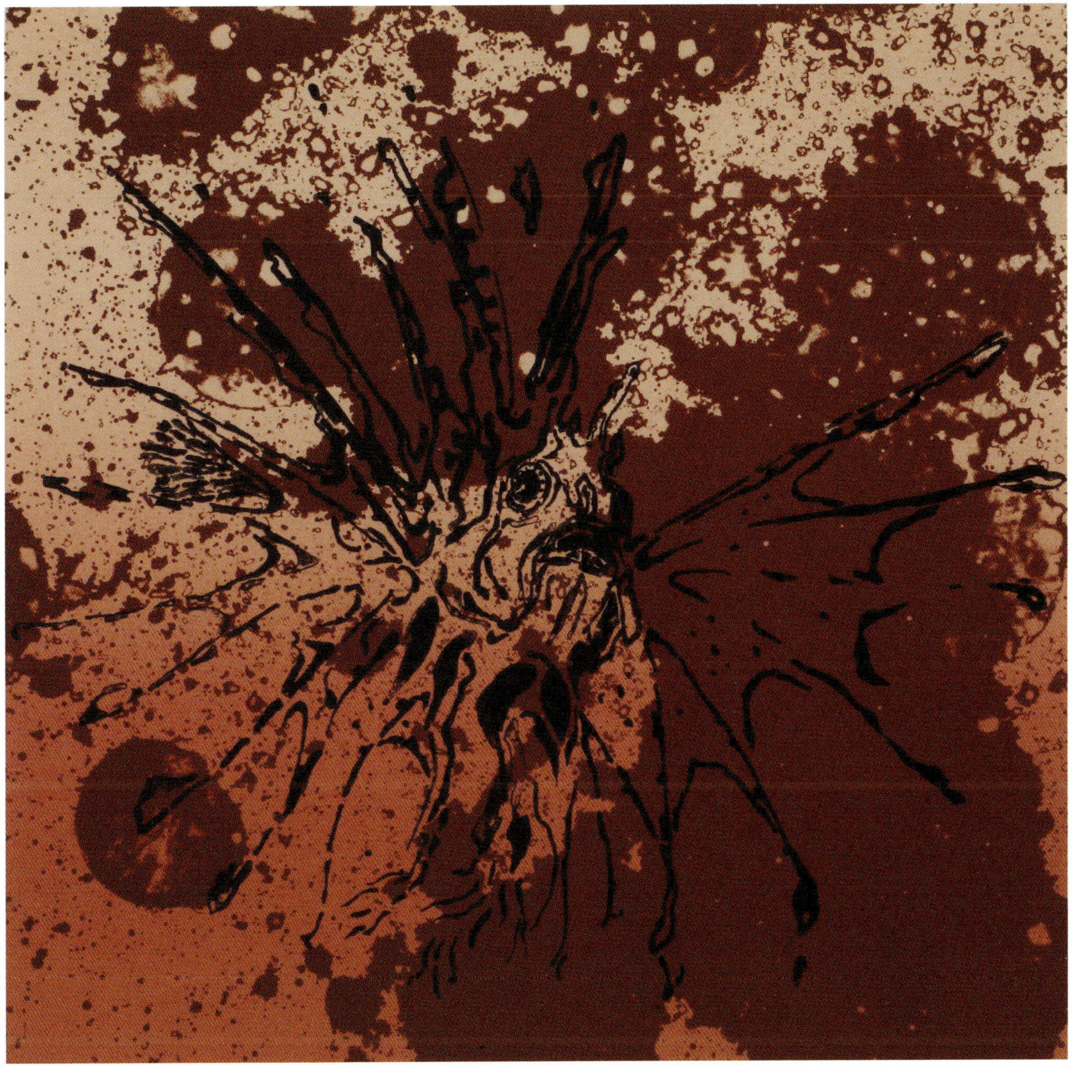

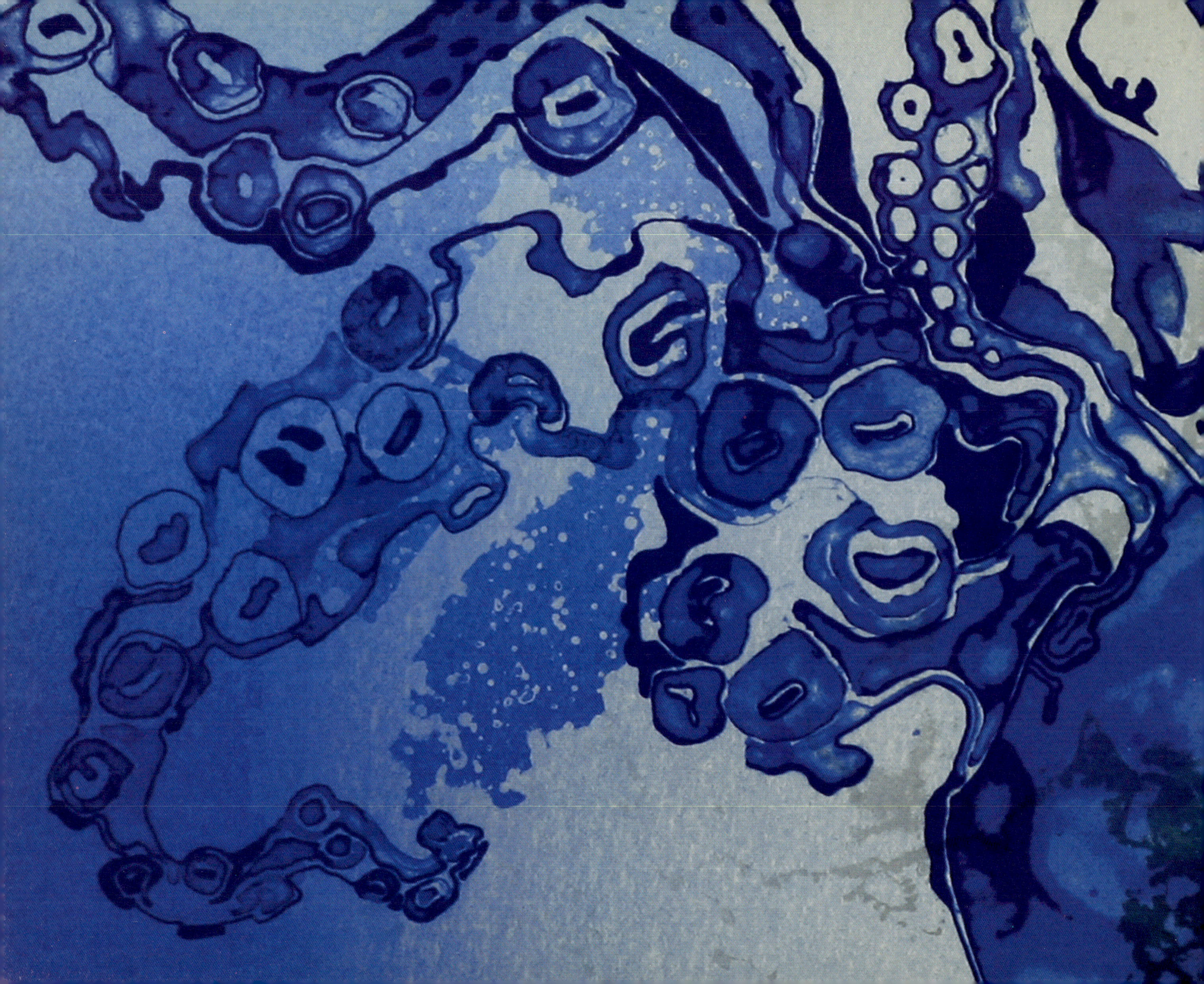

Shhh

Then, it was natural
to hear the sea remembered
in those stony airlocks and chambers
though I soon knew it might as well
be anything – forest fires, landslides,
hurricanes
falsified by distance
or amplification; the white noise
of the wilder elements

or the mild chaos
as she puts her lips to your ear
and you cock your brain to catch
her general drift – the blandishments,
the breath drawn at your touch:
I no longer believe what I hear.

Don Paterson

Proteus
detail
(see p. 37)

From *Nil Nil*, Faber and Faber, 1993

Coming Up For Air
Hand-printed silkscreen print
image size: 30.5 × 30.5 cm; 12 × 12 in
paper size: 52.5 × 50 cm; 21.5 × 19.5 in

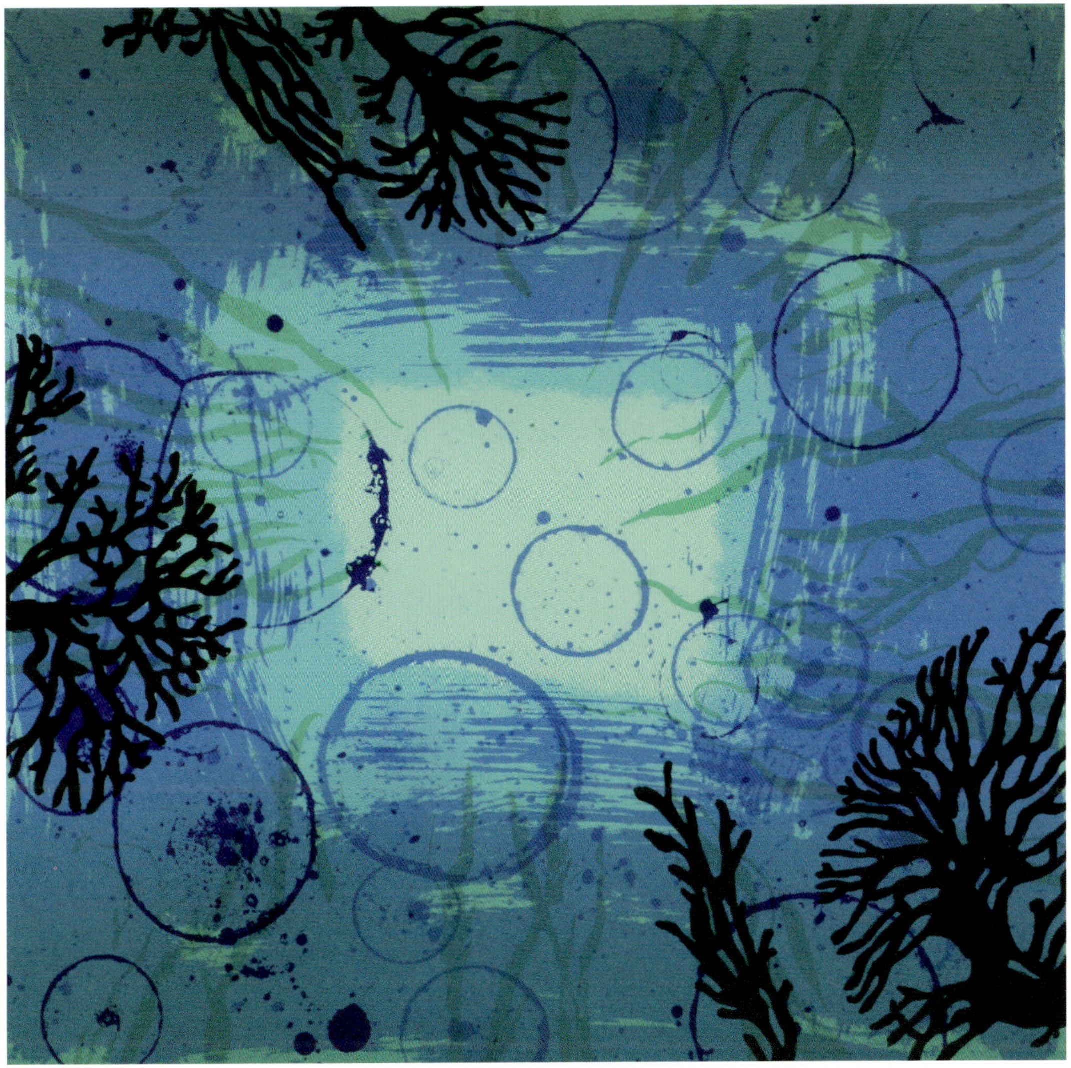

The Merman

He was ploughing his single furrow
Through the green, heavy sward
Of water. I was sowing winter wheat
At the shoreline, when our farms met.

Not a furrow, quite, I argued.
Nothing would come of his long acre
But breaker growing out of breaker,
The wind-scythe, the rain-harrow.

Had he no wish to own such land
As he might plough round in a day?
What of friendship, love? Such qualities?

He remembered these same fields of corn or hay
When swathes ran high along the ground,
Hearing the cries of one in difficulties.

Paul Muldoon

From *Mules*, Faber and Faber, 1977

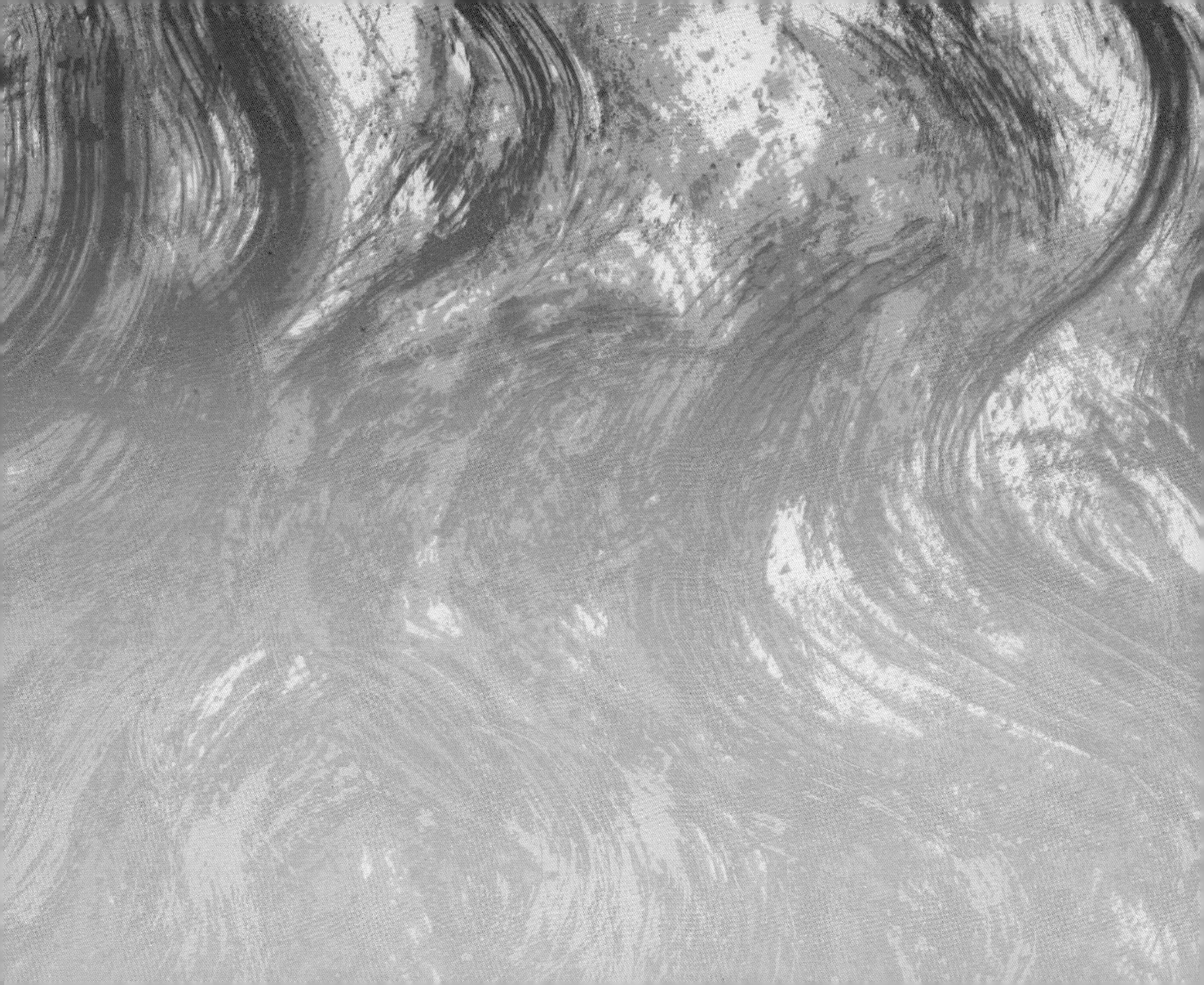

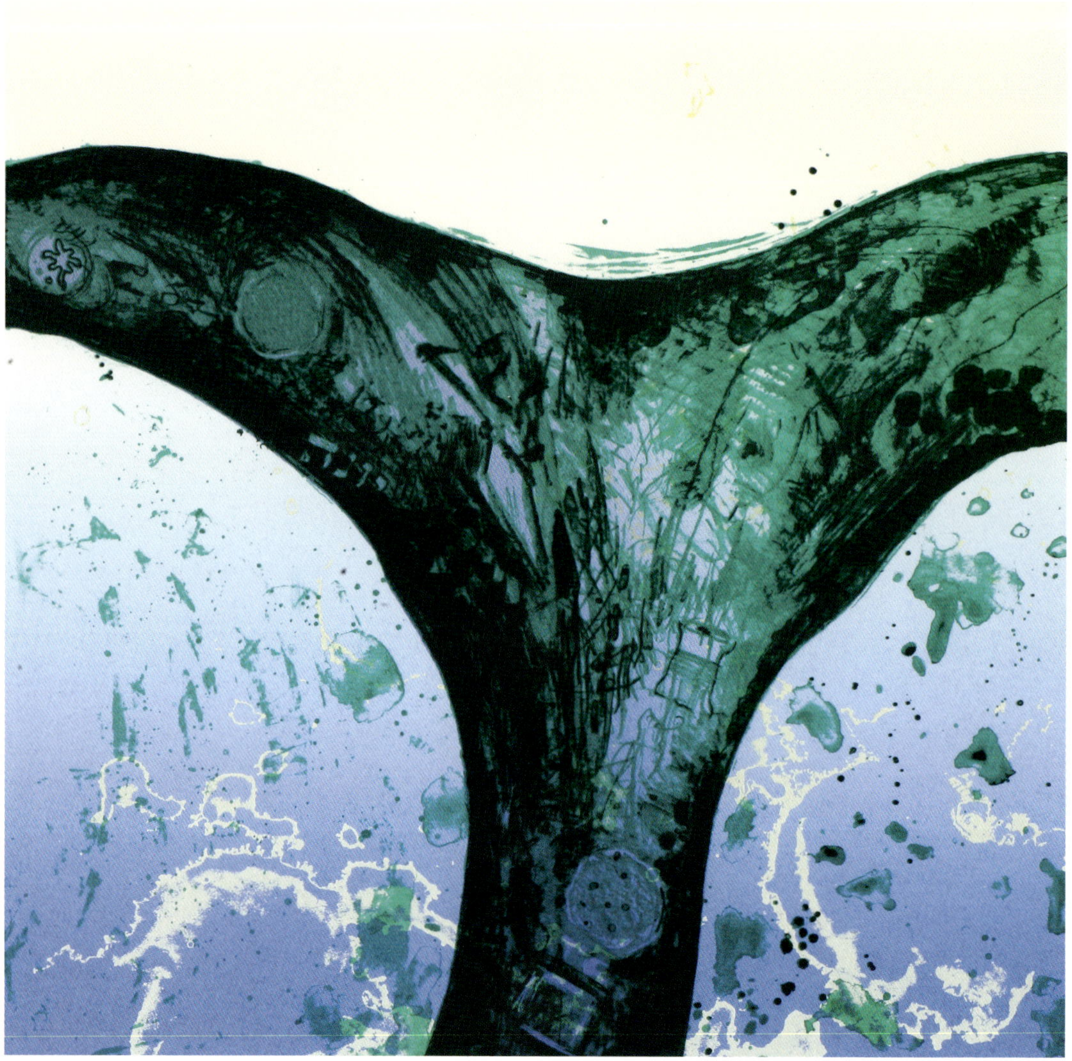

The Comber

A moment before the comber turns into
A breaker – sea spray, raggedy rainbows –
Water and sunlight contain all the colours
And suspend between Inishbofin and me
The otter, and thus we meet, without my scent
In her nostrils, the uproar of my presence,
My unforgivable shadow on the sand –
Even if this is the only sound I make.

Michael Longley

Fluke
Hand-printed silkscreen print
image size: 30.5 × 30.5 cm; 12 × 12 in
paper size: 52.5 × 50 cm; 21.5 × 19.5 in

From *The Weather in Japan*, Jonathan Cape, 2000

Proteus
Hand-printed silkscreen print
image size: 30.5 × 30.5 cm; 12 × 12 in
paper size: 52.5 × 50 cm; 21.5 × 19.5 in

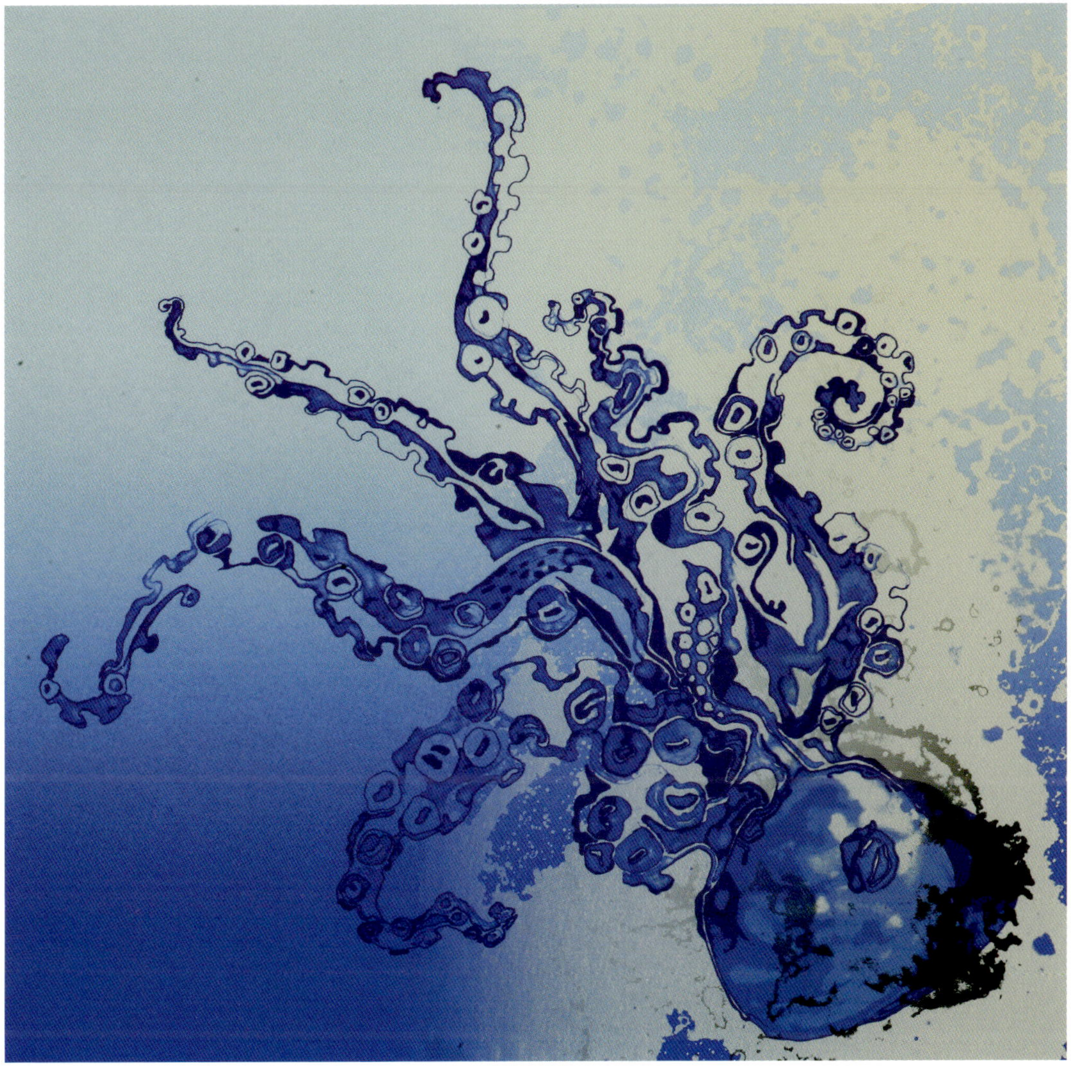

Underwavebreak
Hand-printed silkscreen print
image size: 30.5 × 30.5 cm; 12 × 12 in
paper size: 52.5 × 50 cm; 21.5 × 19.5 in

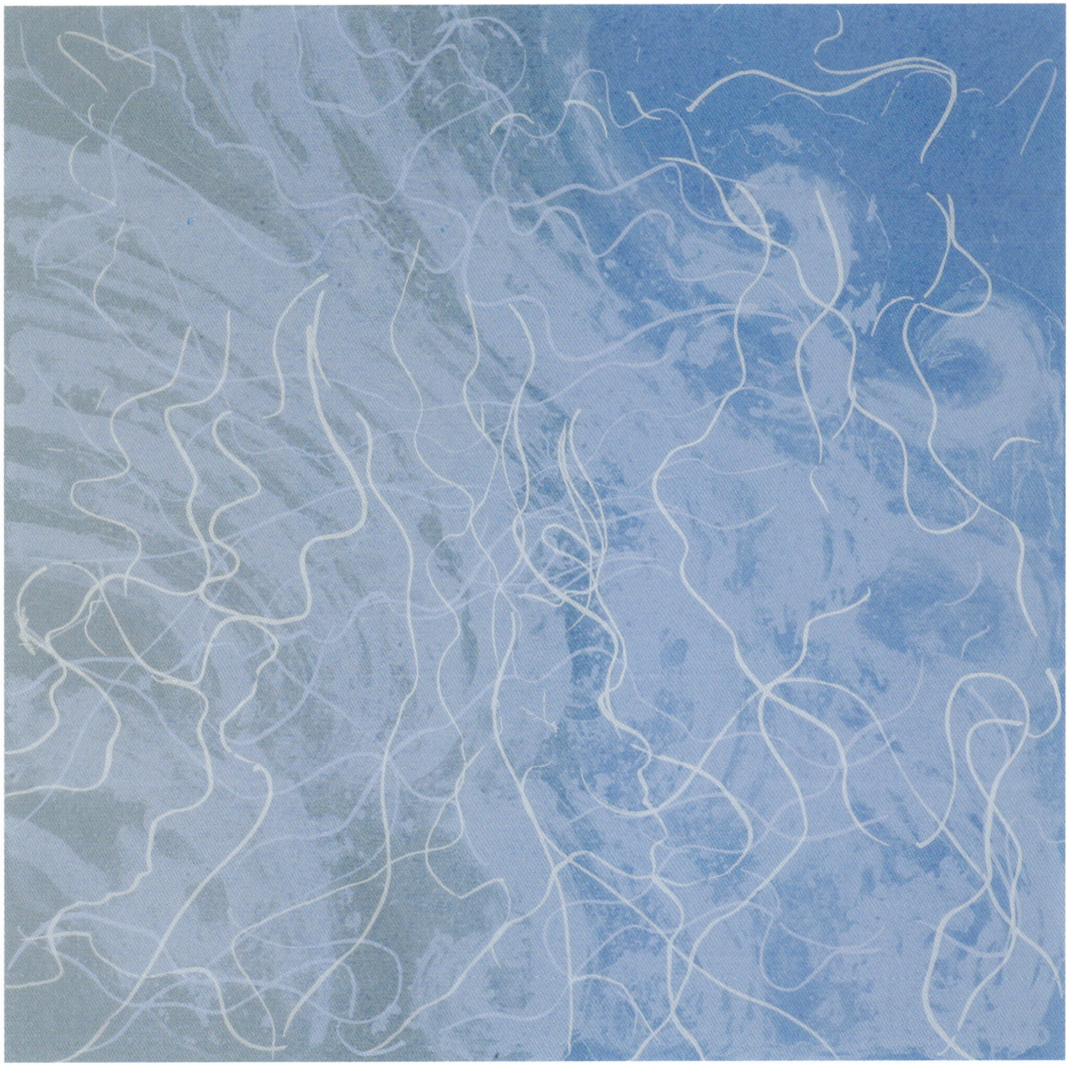

Primrose And Ultramarine
Hand-printed silkscreen print
image size: 30.5 × 30.5 cm; 12 × 12 in
paper size: 52.5 × 50 cm; 21.5 × 19.5 in

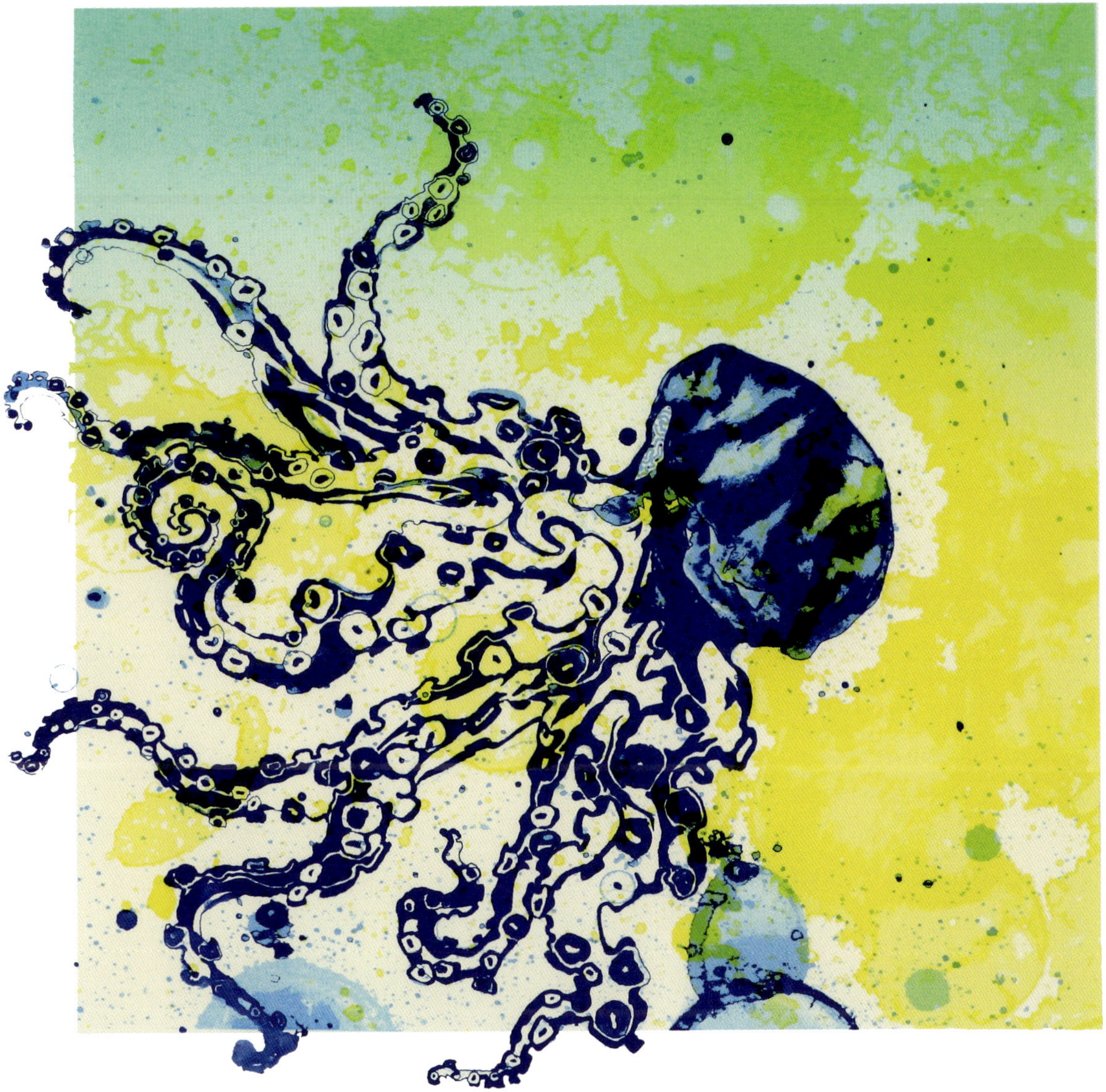

The White Ship

Where the living with effort go,
Or with expense, the drowned wander
Easily: seaman
And king's son also

Who, by gross error lost,
Drift, now, in salt crushed
Polyp-and mackerel-fleshed
Tides between coast and coast,

Submerge or half-appear.
This does not much matter.
They are put down as dead. Water
Silences all who would interfere;

Retains, still, what it might give
As casually as it took away:
Creatures passed through the wet sieve
Without enrichment or decay.

Geoffrey Hill

Breakwater
detail
(see p. 45)

From *For The Unfallen*, André Deutsch, 1968

Breakwater
Hand-printed silkscreen print
image size: 30.5 × 30.5 cm; 12 × 12 in
paper size: 52.5 × 50 cm; 21.5 × 19.5 in

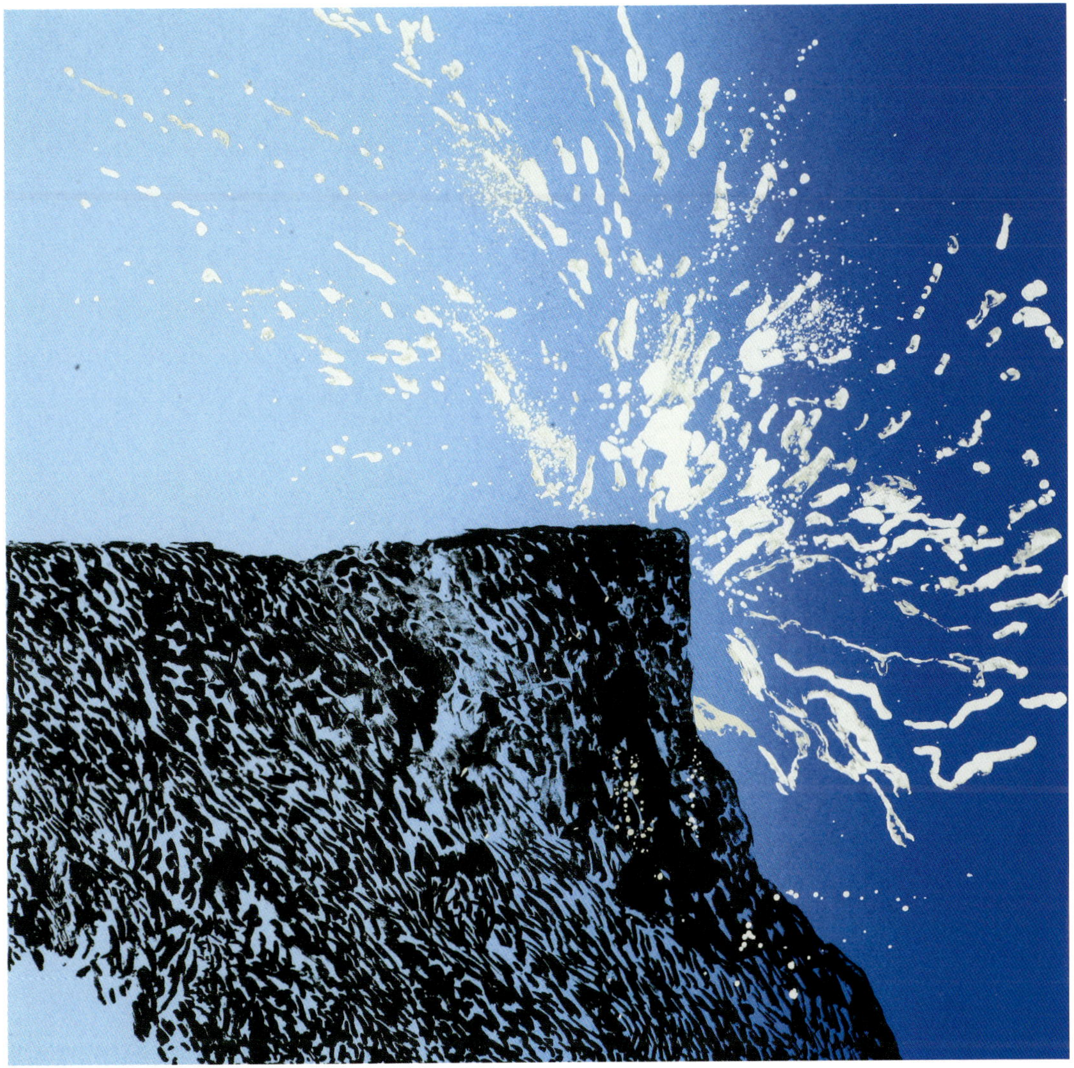

The Water's Edge

Croupier waves flip shells on the downwash
lit, briefly, before they spin and land
you see them lift and topple on the sand,
tokens of the ocean's suspiration.
Smooth-lapped this eastern strand, the border breath
see-saws, ups each addition
then, finger-on-lip, sighs subtraction
as though each retreat were a little death.

Now the faint easterly has dropped
an Optimist fleet floats still beyond
the thin line of islands, divided
like a measuring bar. Molten-cast on
water the sun blazes bulb-white filigree
brighter than Turner, more than one can see.

Ardyn Halter

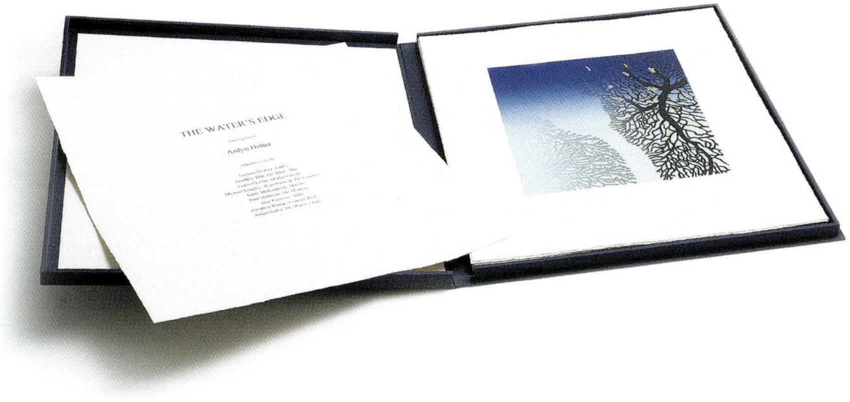
THE WATER'S EDGE
Ardyn Halter

Print details

Image size: 30.5 × 30.5 cm; 12 × 12 in
Paper size: 52.5 × 50 cm; 21.75 × 19.75 in

Edition: 75
10 artist's proofs, 1 insurance proof and 2 printers' proofs

The prints are on 400 gsm Arches paper
The poems are printed on 300 gsm Arches paper

All the prints were made in the Advanced Graphics studio in London
working with Robert Saich, Scott Campbell and Cameron Lindo

The bound boxes were made by Book Works, London

Exhibitions
The British Library, London
La Fortezza, Montalcino, Tuscany
The Horace Richter Gallery, Old Jaffa

Medusa
detail
(see p. 14)

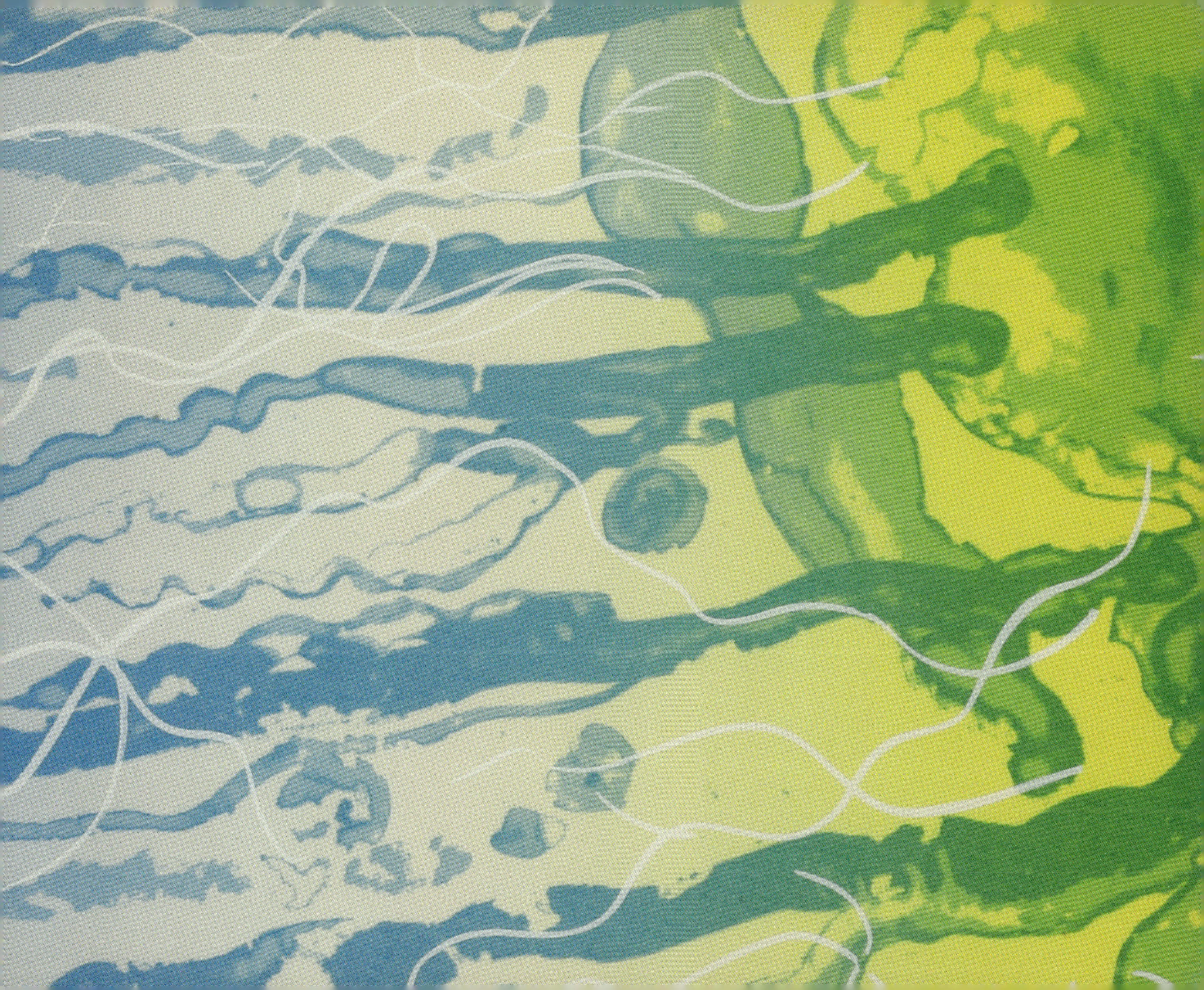

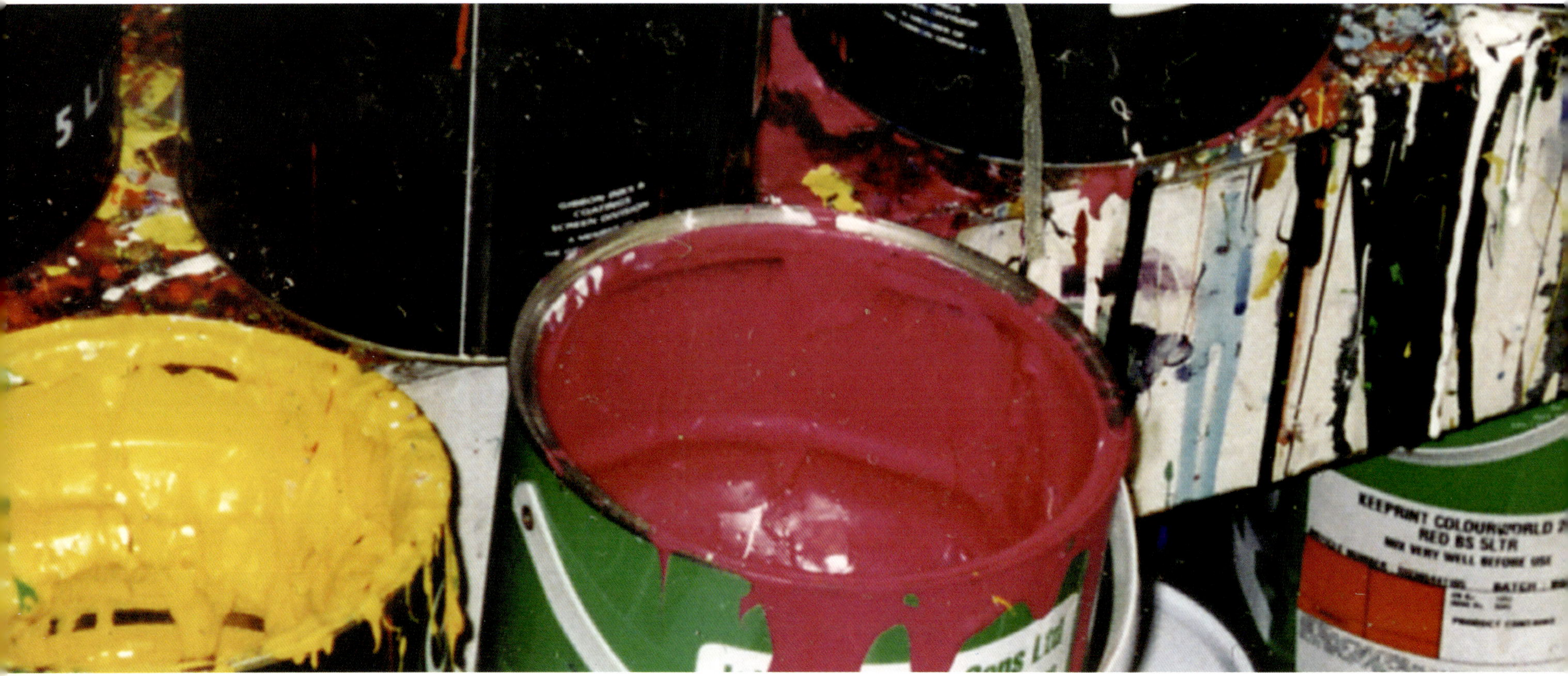
5L
KEEPRINT COLOURWORLD
RED BS SLTR
MIX VERY WELL BEFORE USE
Sons Ltd

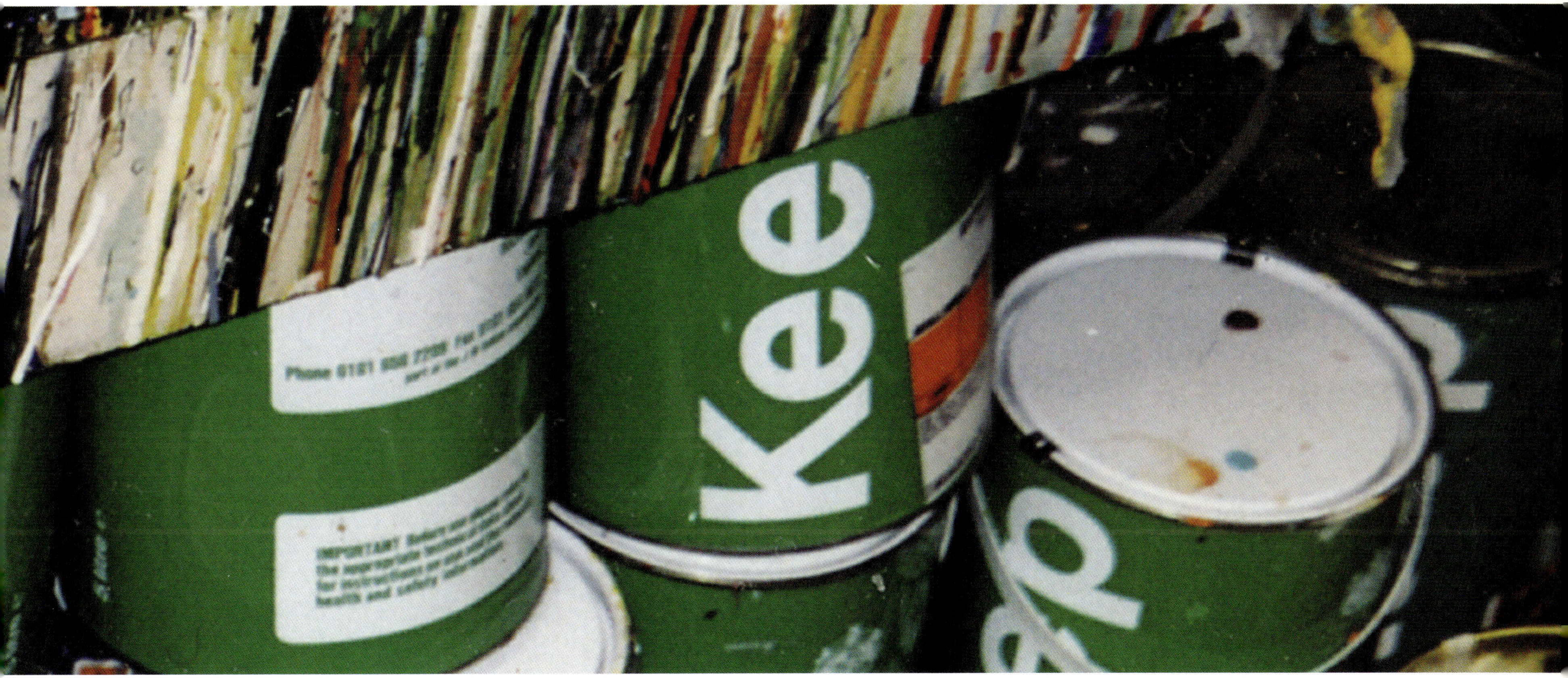
Kee

Part Two

Notes, proofs, drafts and sketches

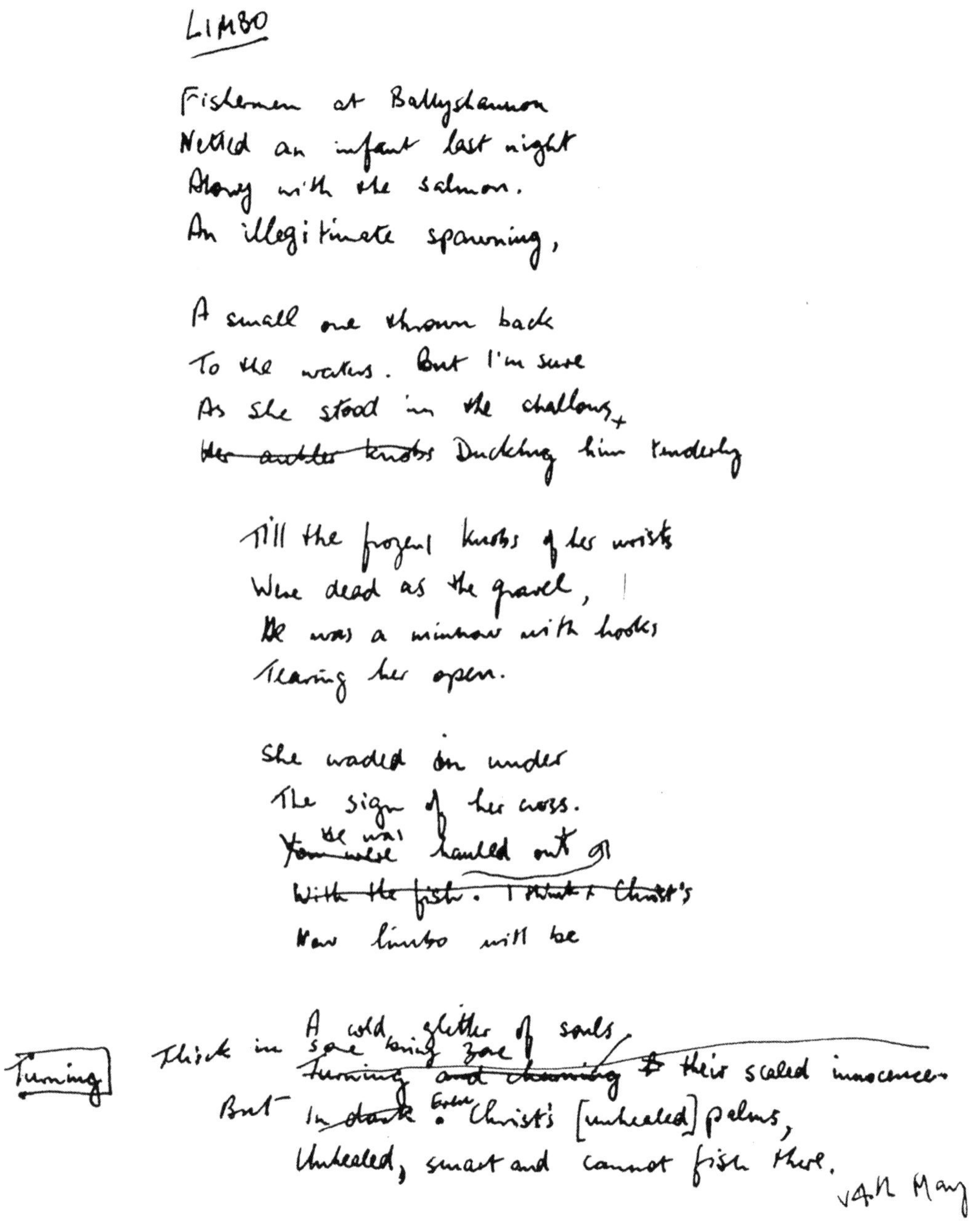

LIMBO

Fishermen at Ballyshannon
Netted an infant last night
Along with the salmon.
An illegitimate spawning,

A small one thrown back
To the waters. But I'm sure
As she stood in the shallows,
~~Her ankles knobs~~ Ducking him tenderly

Till the frozen knobs of her wrists
Were dead as the gravel,
He was a minnow with hooks
Tearing her open.

She waded in under
The sign of her cross.
~~You were~~ He was hauled out
~~With the fish. I think Christ's~~
Now limbo will be

A cold glitter of souls
Thick in some lonely zone ~~Turning and churning~~ their scaled innocence
But In ~~dark~~ Even Christ's [unhealed] palms,
Unhealed, smart and cannot fish there.

Turning

4th May

Seamus Heaney, *Limbo* (see p. 20)

28 December 2003

Dear Ardyn Halter

Thanks for sending that handsome prospectus and news of the British Library exhibition. The whole project is a lovely thorough action. I hope to get to see it in the library.

Meanwhile, I'm sending you a photocopy of a page from an old ledger. There had been an ealier version of "Limbo" but during a week in May 1969 I did a lot of poems very quickly and buffed "Limbo" into final shape some time between 11.00 p.m. on 14 May and 2.00 a.m. on 15th. (There are times noted on a couple of the surrounding pages).

Incidentally, the poem was prompted by a news report on the front page of (I think) The Irish Press, but I changed the location - not thinking of how the people of Ballyshannon might feel.

All good wishes,

Seamus Heaney

These two screens were used in the proofs of *Breakwater* (p. 45) but were removed before the final proofing.

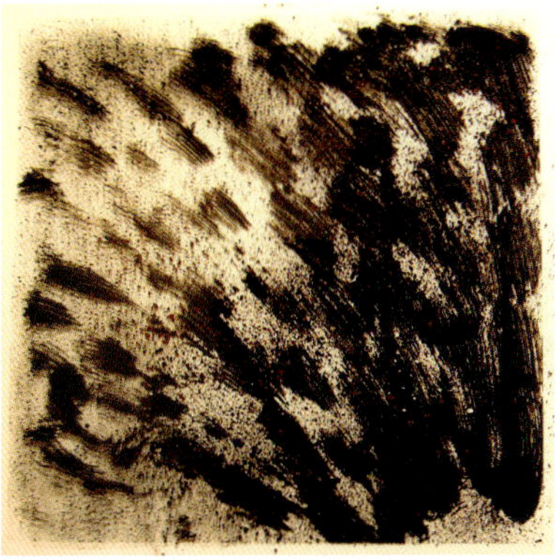

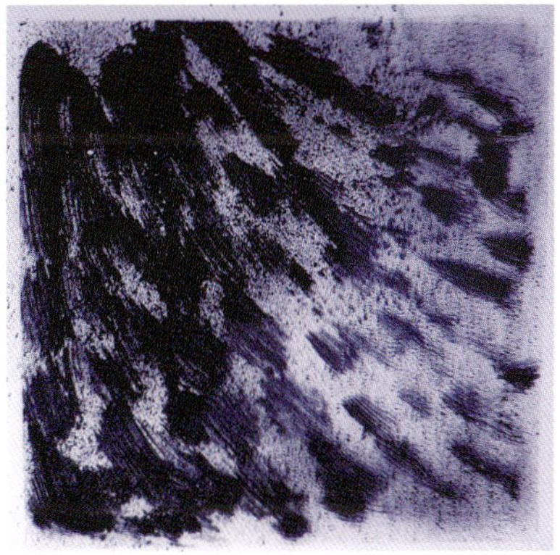

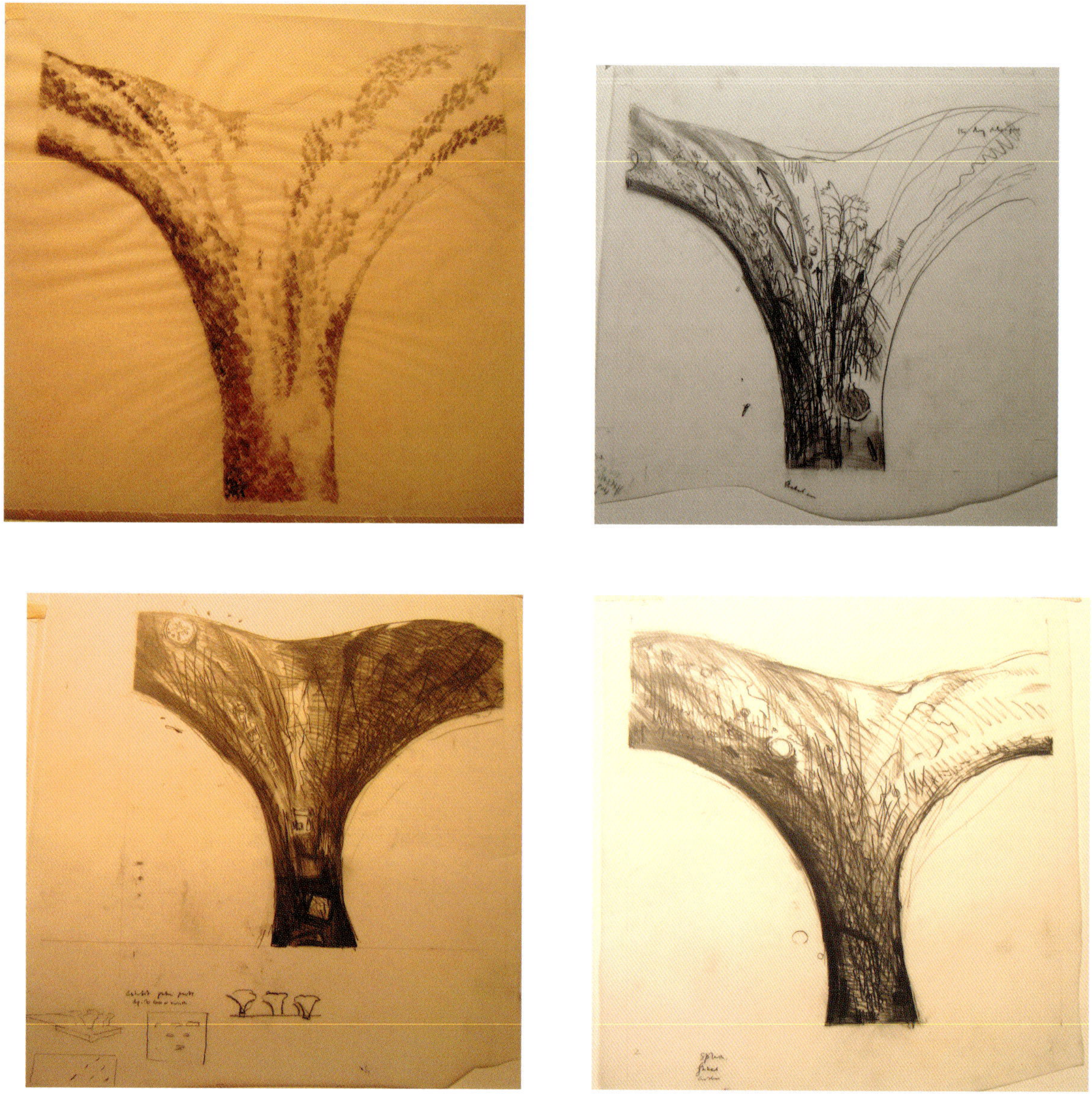

These four sketches and ink washes were made into screens but not used in the final proof of *Fluke* (p. 34).

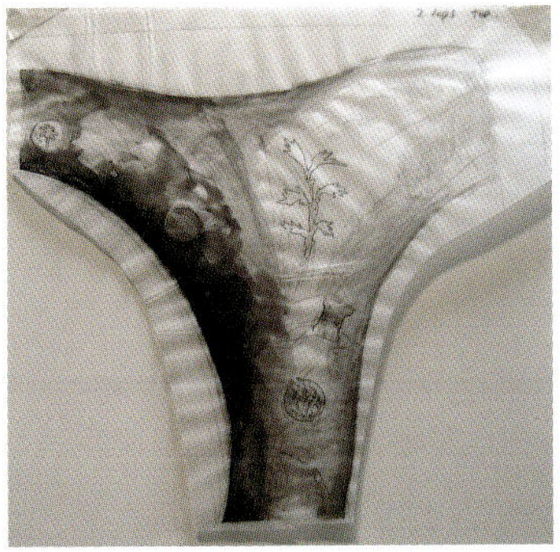

1

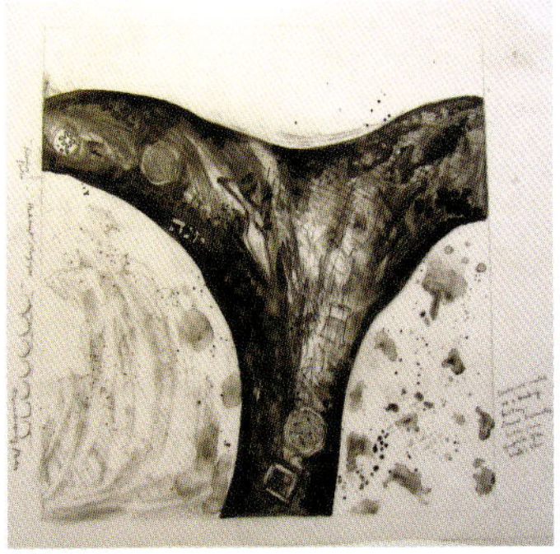

2

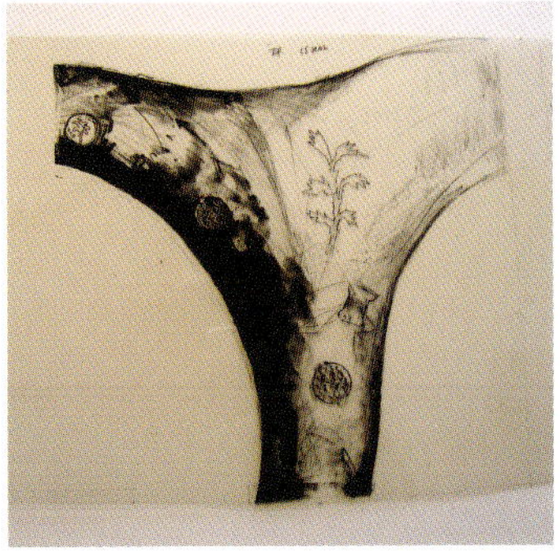

3

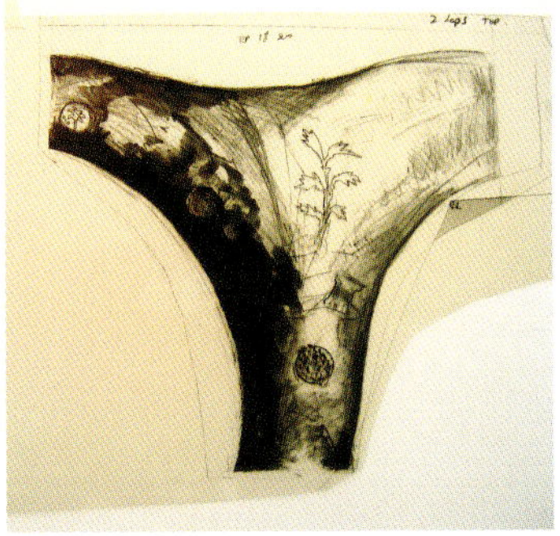

4

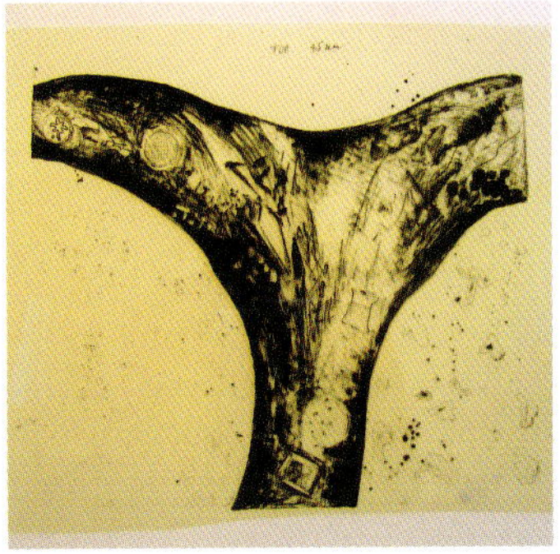

5

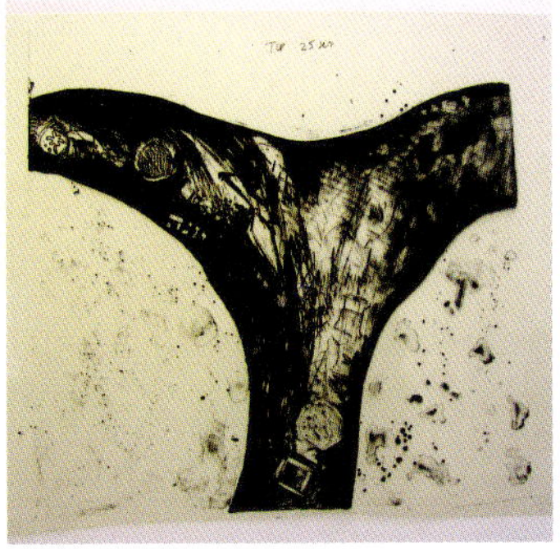

6

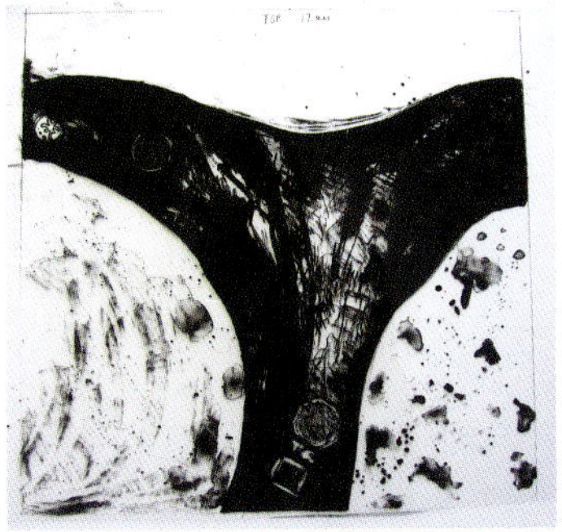

7

2, *5*, *6* and *7* were used in the print *Fluke* (pp. 21 and 34)

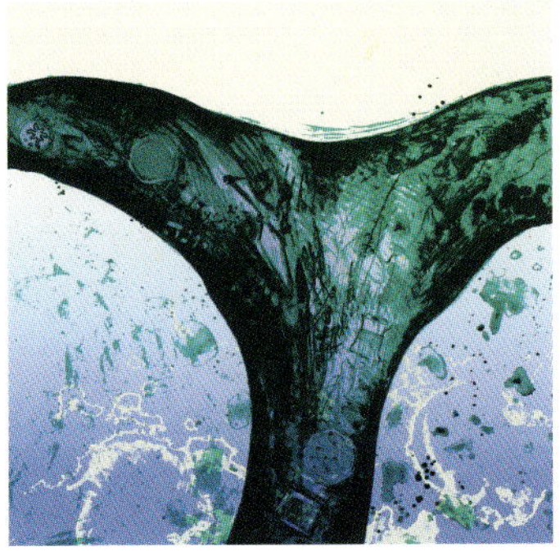

8

Coming Back

(for James Malpas)

When the something withdrawn (you cannot tell
exactly what or when) flows back into the blood
and you return from the damned into your own
(where living is at last to be living now
which the damned cannot know); when your beloved
is again beloved, and morning shows a tree
dressed in light, meaning and memory
at peace in its leaves; when your thought is cool
as linen and you go downstairs to receive
a letter from a friend with total recall
who tells you what you were, and you listen
with attention to rain on the skylight
which tells you what you are;

then you know
that nothing is so lost or gone to waste
that it cannot start again; as when you leave
the city for the pulsing air and the sea
which turns upon itself and fills you, something
bows you down to the ground, bows you weeping
down to the sand, weeping there and giving thanks.

Stephen Romer, *Coming Back* (see p. 24)

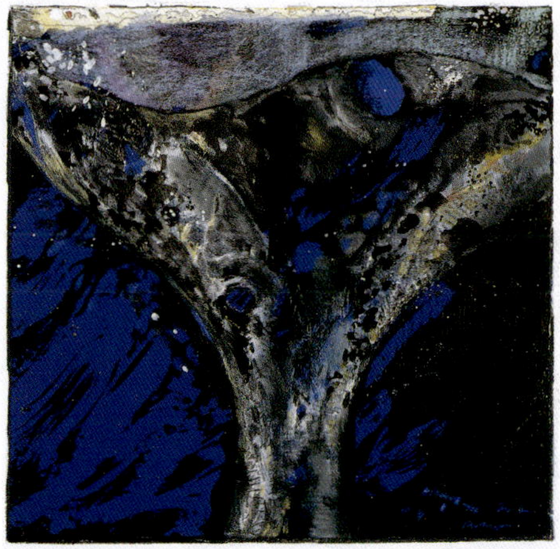

Night Fluke, monoprint with chalk and gouache

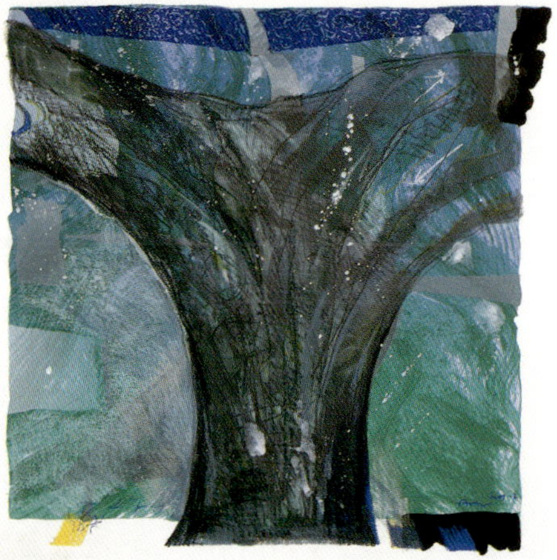

Fluke II, monoprint with pencil and watercolour

Re: Those poems – I really have no jottings about them – in fact they both came rapidly, and were 'given whole', with just a very few amendments. This is true of 'Coming Back' especially, which actually represents a surge of creative energy after frozen months of relative alienation: I remember the sense of release vividly (and the moment on the beach). Eliot's 'lost heart quickens and rejoices' (in fact the whole of 'Ash Wednesday') is germane to my poem, though different in implication.

Stephen Romer (email, 6th March 2004)

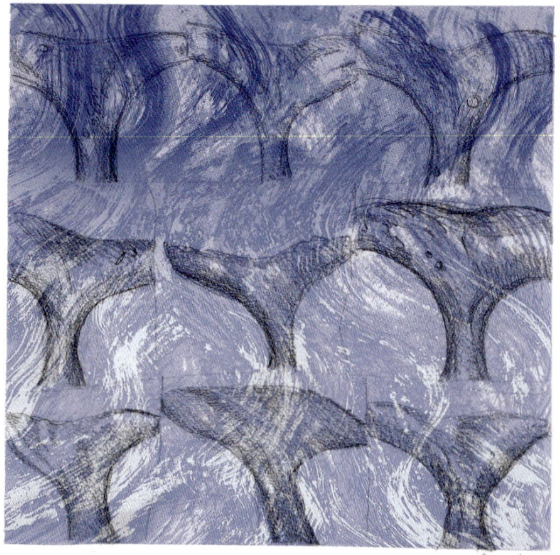

Nine Flukes; *Sargasso* plus pencil sketches

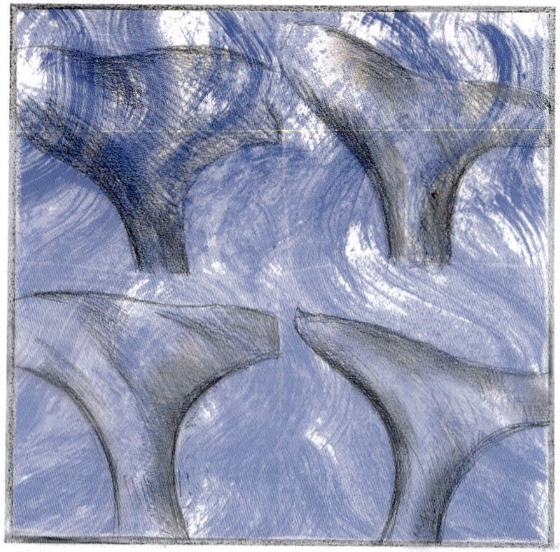

Four Flukes; *Sargasso* plus pencil sketches

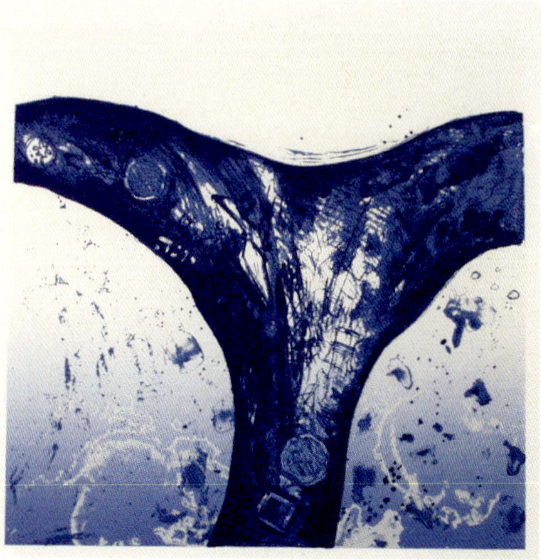

Fluke, blue proof (not used)

Sea Changes

The novices drink and smoke, or stand
on deck, blinded by the rhetoric
of a riding moon with clouds. Our wake
is white, a crumpled parachute
spreading out behind.

Grown used to this journey through the night,
wrapped in a coat, curled on a seat,
I ask only for a heart as constant
as the throbbing of this ship, and strong
for each new sickening of the sea.

Stephen Romer, *Sea Changes*, Oxford University Press, 1986

A Second Note

To what extent does a poet visualize what he or she is writing? How far does an artist verbalize his images in the process of making them and after they are made? I suspect that the former do so more than the latter. Poets visualize their work more than painters verbalize theirs (apart from conceptual art which, with few exceptions, requires a sustaining safety net of verbiage).

How far did an image of a young woman wading into the cold sea, carrying her infant, steer the words of Seamus Heaney's poem *Limbo*? He writes that the poem was prompted by a paragraph in a newspaper. That itself is a form of image. I think that an intensely physical visualization is at work there, powerfully grounding, anchoring Heaney's poetry to a physical reality, a place visualized from the world, as well as a composite image mined from a physical seam in his imagination.

Or the conch in Don Paterson's poem *Shhh*: at what point did the hand holding the shell cease to be a visualization of a hand holding a shell to an ear and become pre-eminently the sound and order of words?

In Geoffrey Hill's *The White Ship*, although it is not mentioned, the black sail is always – in my mind as reader – before my eyes as much as before my ears as I reread the poem. To what extent is the image of the ship defined by Hill's words? Indeed at what moment does it cease to be a visual image and become an auditory one? Not just for the reader but for the poet too. And is it in the foreground or the background that we sense it? And do these poems conjure up visual images of disparate intensity in the minds of the readers? I suppose that they must. We are different and see things differently with our eyes and with our mind's eye.

So did most of these poems start with words or with images? Does imagination separate the two? Which of them does the brain trigger more quickly – can they be released in tandem? Does sight strike the flint or is it sound? Is the image sparked with the speed of light, and do smoke and flames only then spread outwards like sound waves? Even as I write this I am employing images to express this idea. A word that triggers verbal associations, itself sounds off something. The inner sound-waves reflect off objects, physically real things and places stored (for me) in my visual memory. We each carry with us rooms and houses, faces, gardens, seascapes, landscapes, the accreted

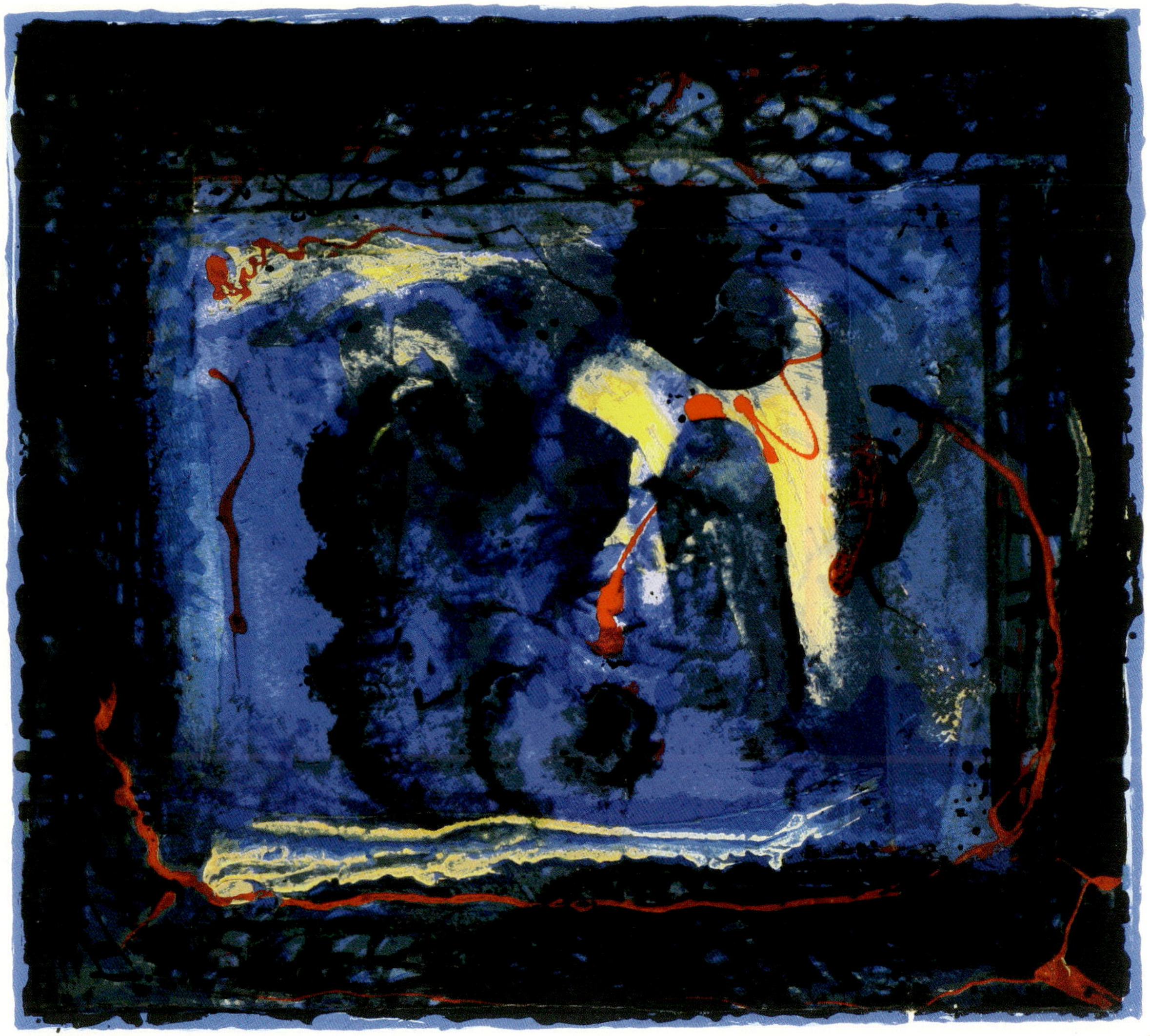

Water, Swimming into Morning, silkscreen and woodblock print, 1996–7 (edition of 95). Size: 87 × 92.5 cm; 35 × 37 in

world of our lives stored there in memory in different degrees of incompleteness.

A thing, a poem, may set off with an image, yet find its truest expression in words. Yet to what degree do those words, carried by sound, by the intonations, stress, metre, rhyme, the breath of thought then return redefined as a different image? Its essential existence is in words and breath, but is it only so? Or has it also a new existence of a different visual nature?

All my prints, all my paintings, started their path as visual images. Most of my prints continued, consciously, as lists of words, ideas notated in words, ideas I did not wish to put into image lest I confine the spontaneity of their generation in the print studio. For the greatest gift of the print studio and of the process of proofing is the hap image, the chance tangent that leads you in unforeseen directions, paths you would not take if you confined yourself to a preconceived image. From lists of verbalized ideas, the images then evolved in a process that was purely visual. All that mattered was colour and decisions of a purely visual order. Words became irrelevant to them, though the process of their making were ideas sketched out as words.

Association of words, do these come before images in the making of a poem? These words, all words, echo off a place. Gabriel Levin's poetry sounds off the Levantine shore to the extent that his draft of the poem *Mediterranean* has a map of the coast from Joppa to Tel Sukar with the island of Cyprus poking its north east promontory like a marlinspike into the last line of the sonnet. A jabbing awareness that cartographical reality provides an unseen physical matrix, plotted beneath and within his writing.

Robin Robertson starts squarely on the bleak north-east shore of Scotland. The poem is an inverted sonnet, first the sestet and then the octave. The last line of the sestet talks of what he is seeing, the turning wave, a 'sea valve' turning 'with a shock into sound'. Image becoming sound, the sound pipe music, the Pibroch of the title.

Thinking back, *The Taninim Stream* began with a walk, the sound of a stream, the smell of aniseed flowers and mustard bloom. It then fused with an image of a friend, a man mid-stream, mid-life, water swirling round his ankles. He was not there before I wrote the poem. He came to be physically present.

Paul Muldoon's world of sight appears through apertures of thought in his writing. Its presence is not insistent. There is a teasing dissolution of image into sound. In *Merman*, just as the furrow gains visual form, it dissolves in water, becomes insubstantial, in verbal solution. 'Scythe-wind' and 'rain-harrow' are at once intensely physical and also beyond physicality. One is conscious of the hyphens as agents of linkage and of dissolution, as they work on more than the visual sense in our imagination. Even the title *Merman* – one is conscious of the two syllables. It is distanced from the simple response we have to the word 'mermaid', which would not prompt us to to consider the conjunction of 'mer' and 'maid'. 'Merman' does. Hearing 'Mer', we also hear the sea and think of how we hear the sea in the word 'Mer', and that *sound* plays against the word 'man'. Muldoon intertwines diverse threads of voice and image into an unexpectedly original braid.

Poems illustrate themselves. If a poem makes visual a world or a moment then it does not need either a photograph or an image to illustrate it. If a poem steers away from the visual then it should be allowed to do so unimpeded. None of the images in *The Water's Edge* are illustrations of the poems. None of the poems grew out of the images (though one can think of many examples of poems that have been sparked by a picture). The overlap in this simple Venn diagram is the sea or water. The primary response water elicits is as simple and as immediate as our own physical response when we swim, or our deepest memory of the sea whence we all came, or our oldest memory of amniotic water-burst just before we entered this world.

Ardyn Halter

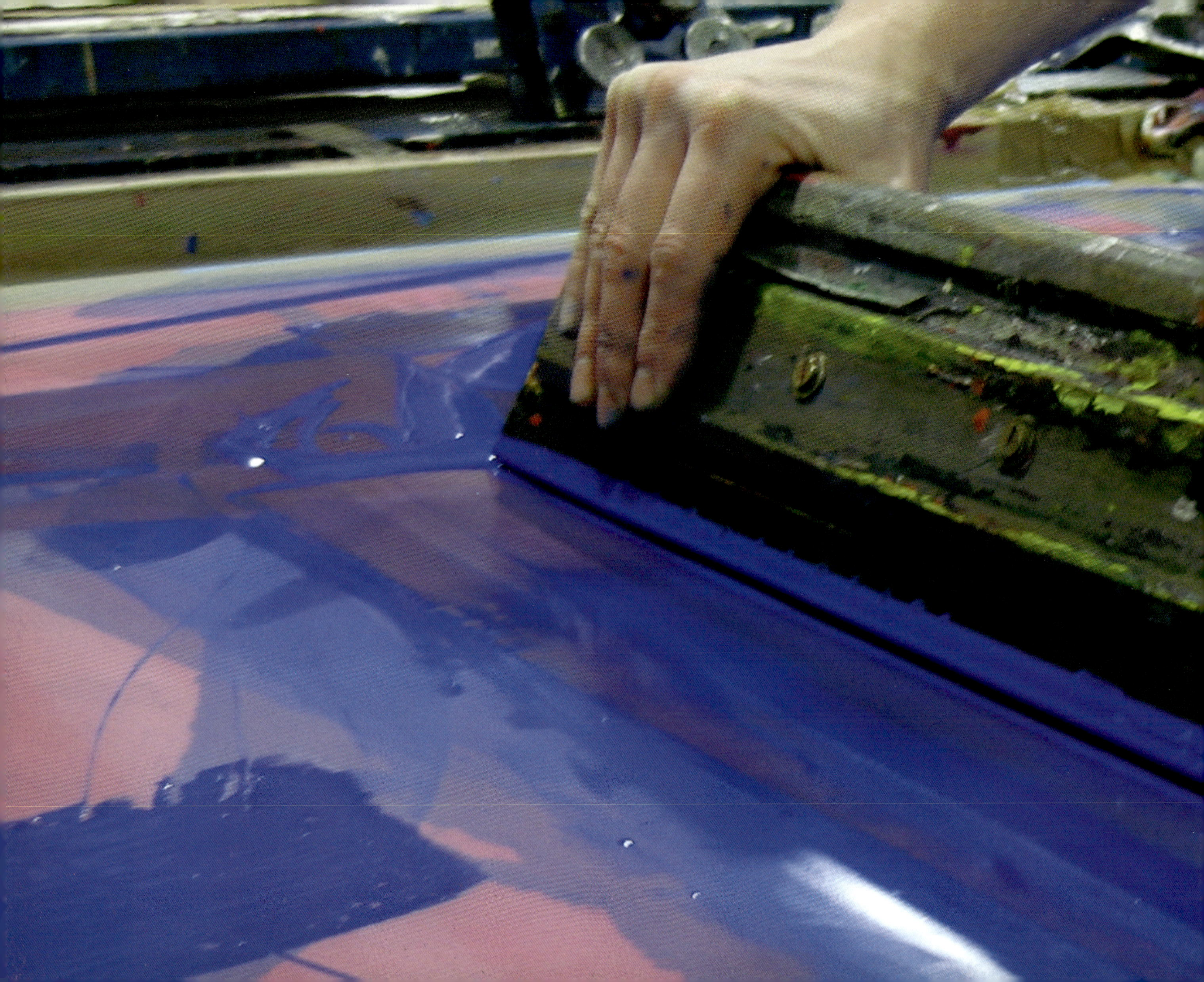

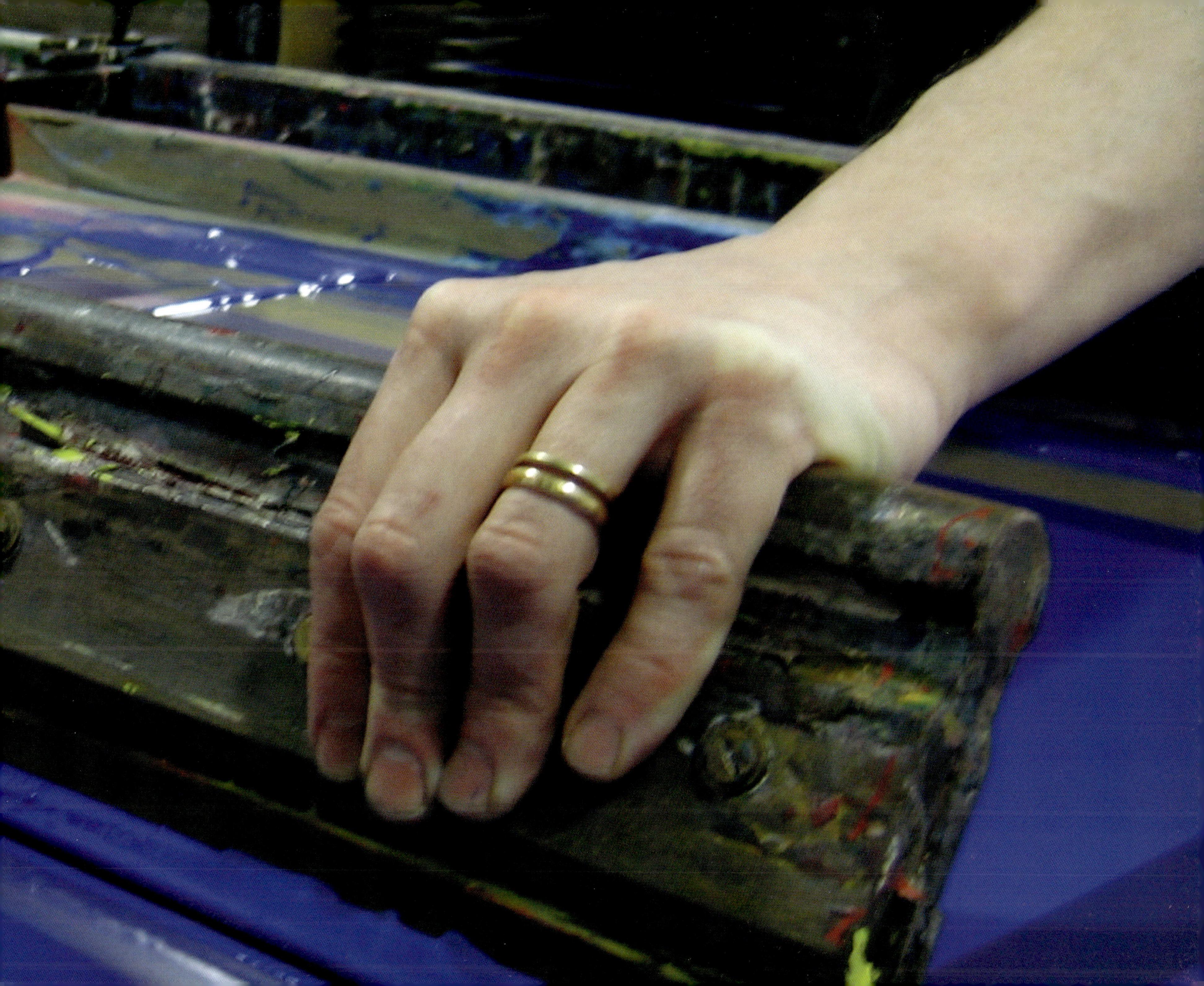

Water-burn

We should have been galloping on horses, their hoofprints
Splashes of light, divots kicked out of the darkness,
Or hauling up lobster pots in a wake of sparks. Where
Were the otters and seals? Were the dolphins on fire?
Yes, we should have been doing more with our lives.

Michael Longley

Full-scale detail of central image on p. 71

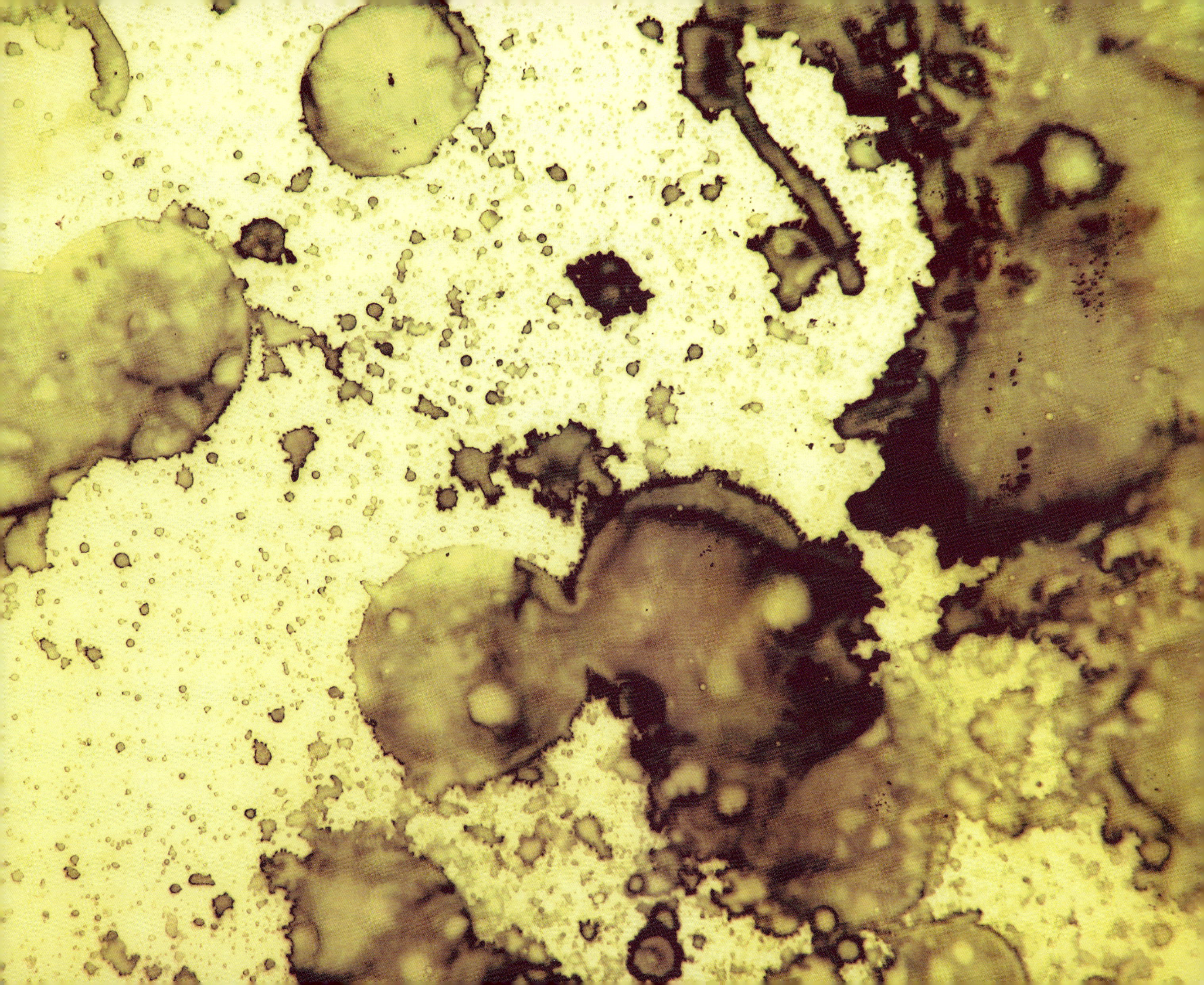

The Comber

A moment before the comber turns into
A breaker – sea-spray, raggedy rainbows –
Water and sunlight contain all the colours
And suspend between Inishbofin and me
The otter, and thus we meet, without my scent
In her nostrils, the uproar of my presence,
My unforgivable shadow on the sand –
Even if this is the only sound I make.

Michael Longley

Michael Longley, *The Comber* (p. 35)

Subject: **poems**
Date: Tue, 06 Jan 2004 13:58:47 +0000

View as HTML

Dear Ardyn Halter,
Than you for your letter of 7 December.
I am pleased to be part of your watery project. Unfortunately my drafts are either illegible or, since I bought a pc, lost in cyberspace. In any case I have always felt superstitious about selfconsciously ordering them. Simply not destroying them seems self-important enough! But I have written out in longhand those two poems and will send these in a cardboard tube to Dickenson Rd - unless you indicate otherwise.
'The Comber' was a happy gift. Did you know that 'water-burn' is Scots for phosphorescence in water? Far richer than standard English. Heaney's 'Limbo' is very beautiful.
Warm wishes,
Michael Longley

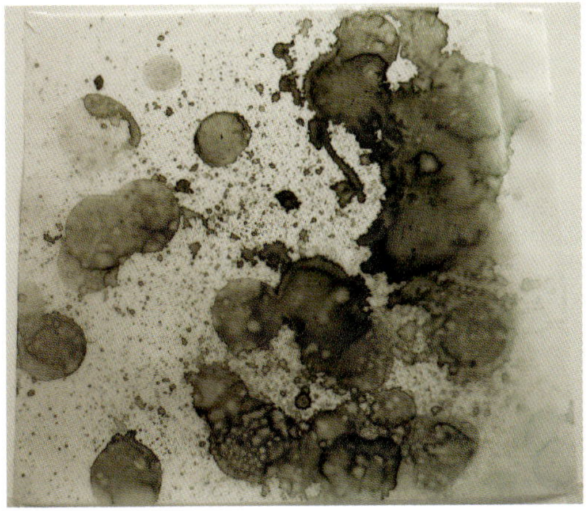

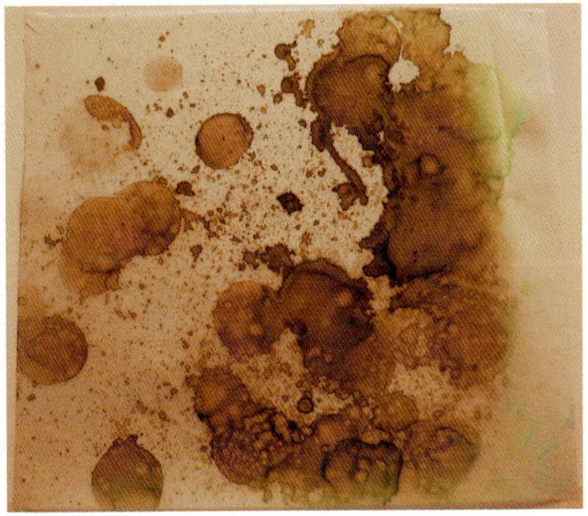

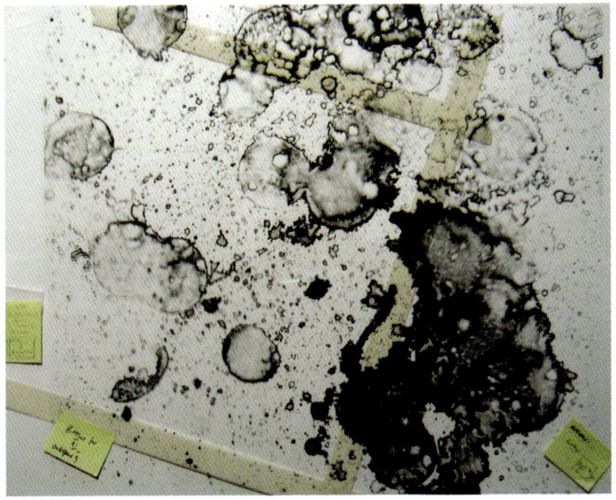

Details of all three images were used from different angles in *Proteus* (pp. 28 and 37) and *Red Sea* (p. 27).

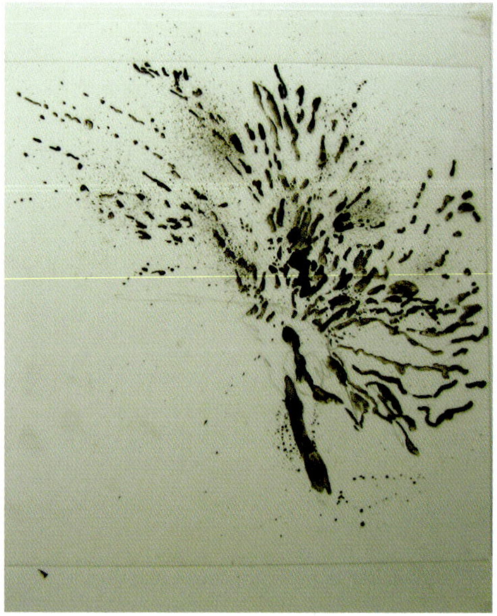

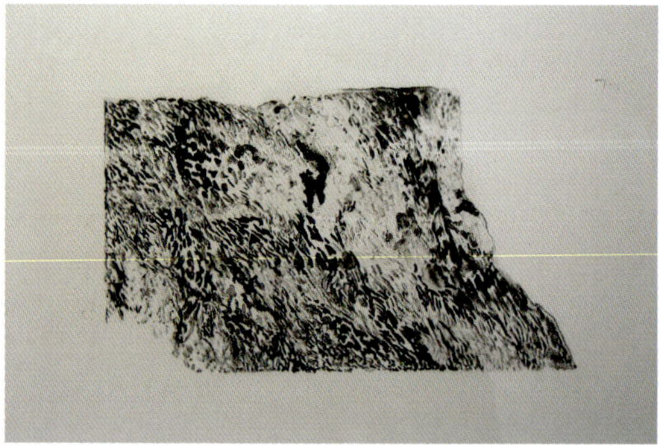

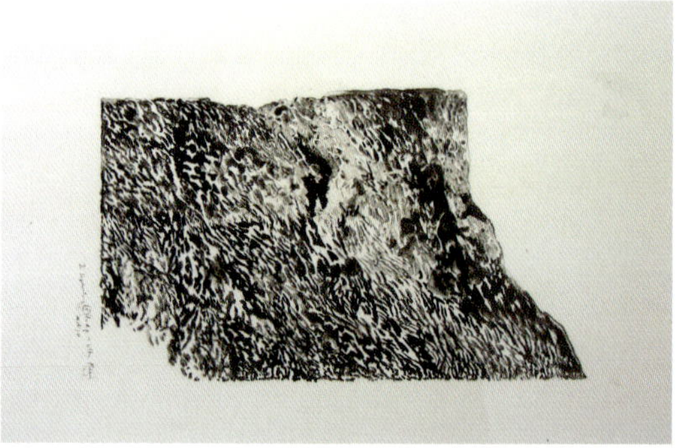

All five elements on this page were used in the proofs and the final print *Breakwater* (pp. 43 and 45).

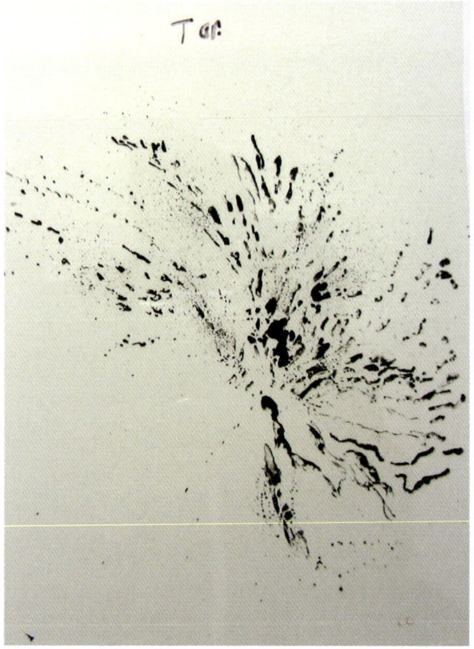

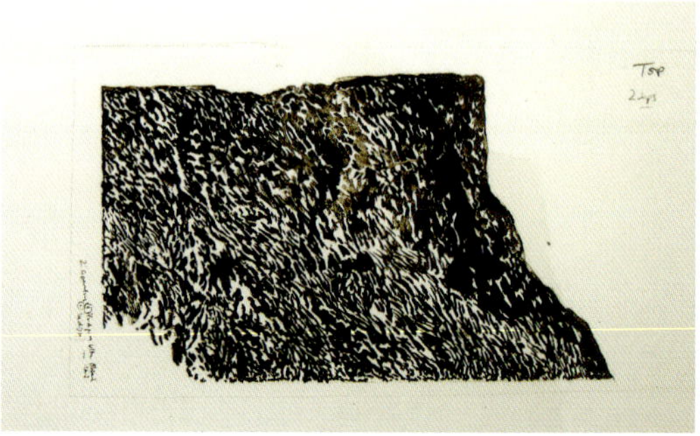

Breakwater, final proofed image (right)

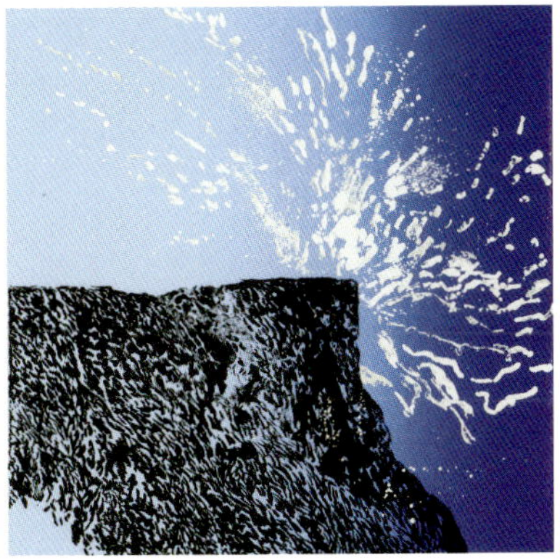

The sketch below was intended for use in *Breakwater* and *Underwavebreak* and a third print that was never realised beyond the early stages of proofing. See full-scale detail, p. 74.

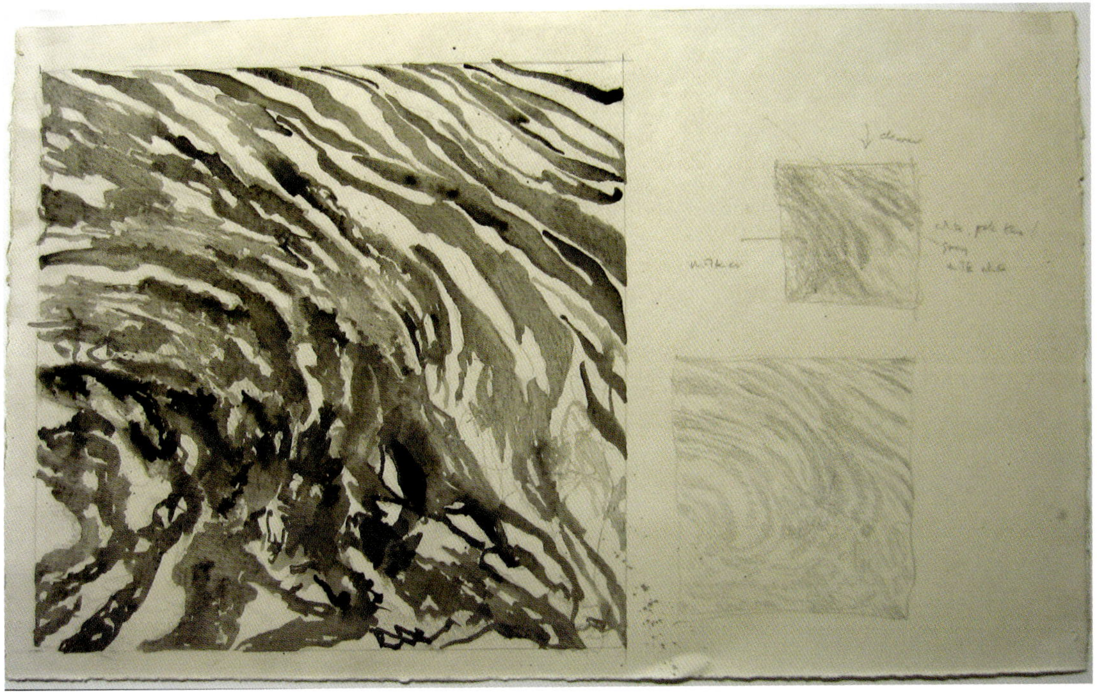

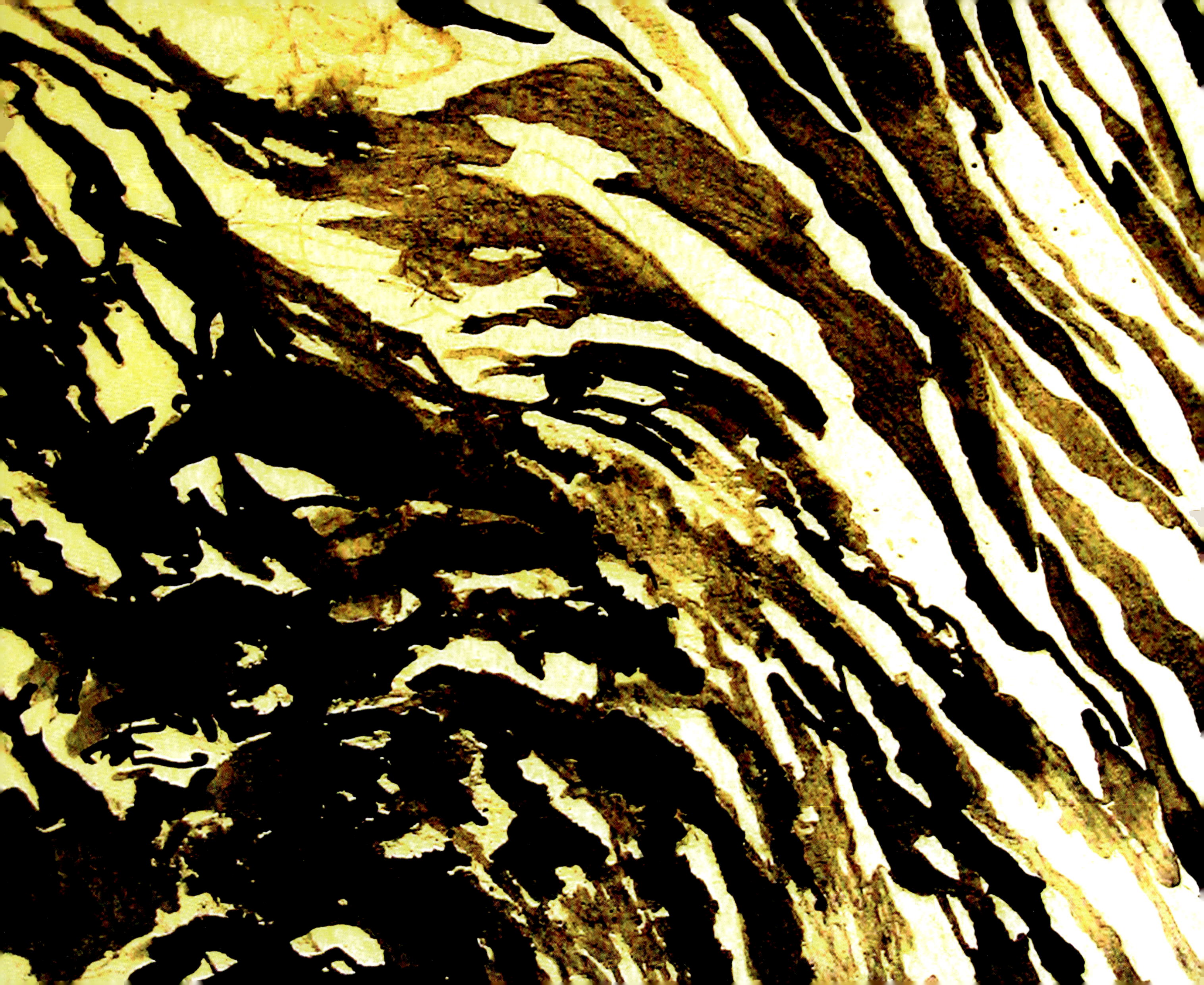

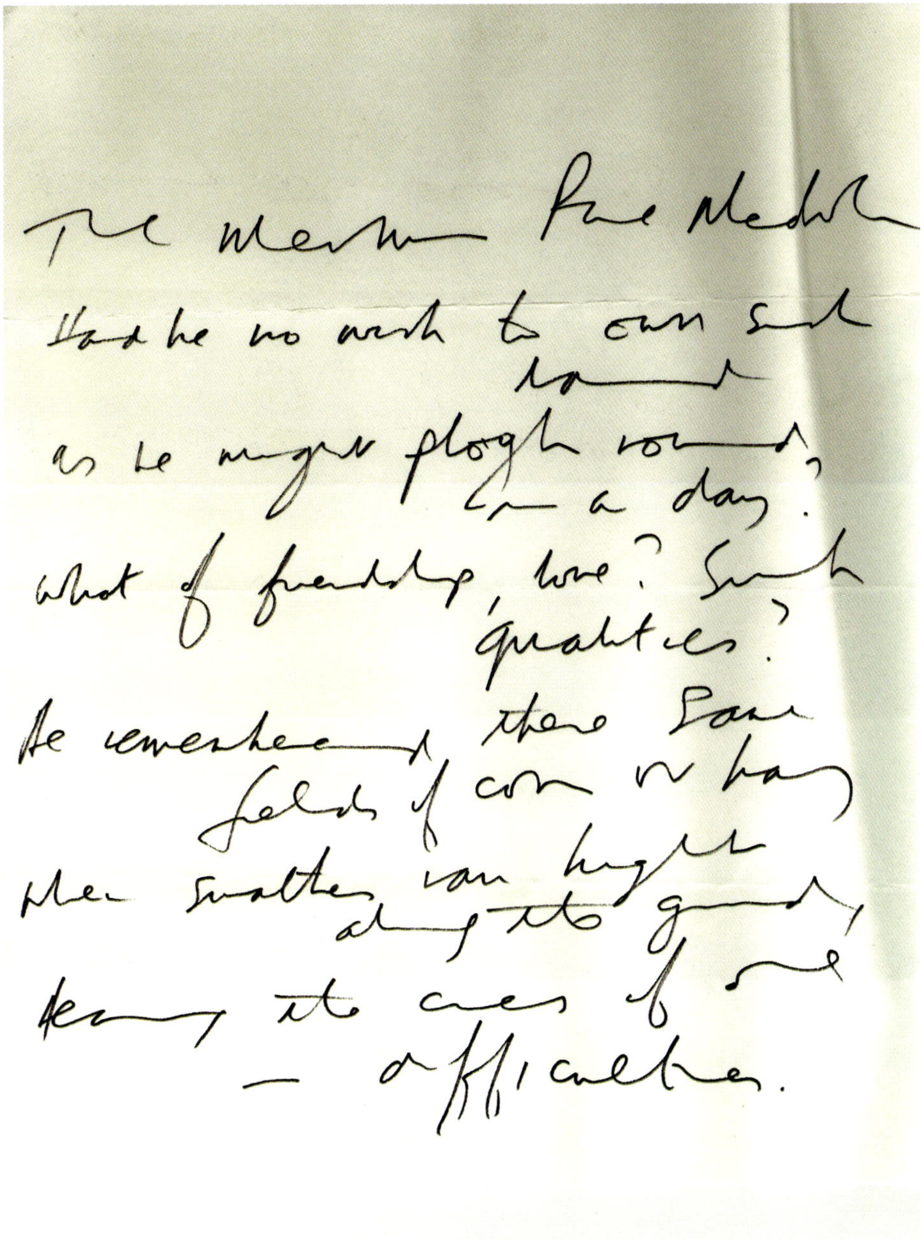
The Merman Paul Muldoon

Had he no wish to own such land
as he might plough round in a day?
What of friendship, love? Such qualities?
He remembered there being fields of corn or hay
when swathes ran higher along the ground,
Hearing its cries of some
— agriculture.

Paul Muldoon, *The Merman* (p. 32)

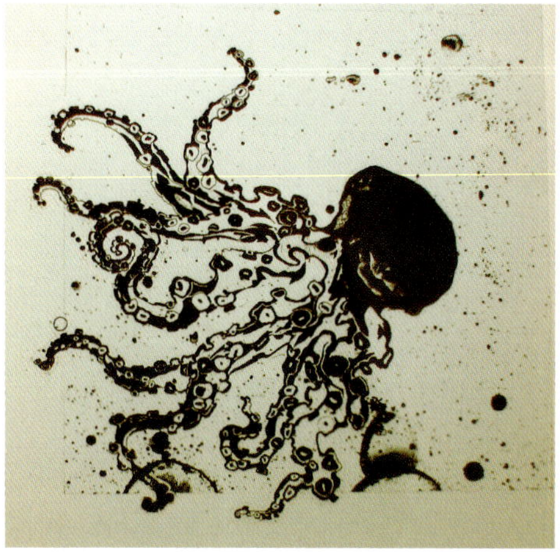

1

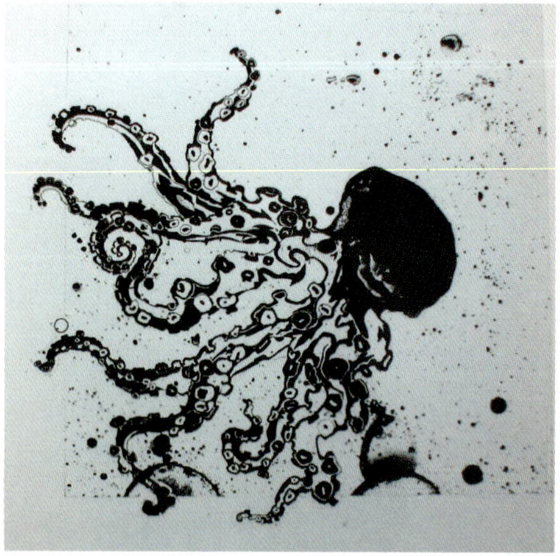

2

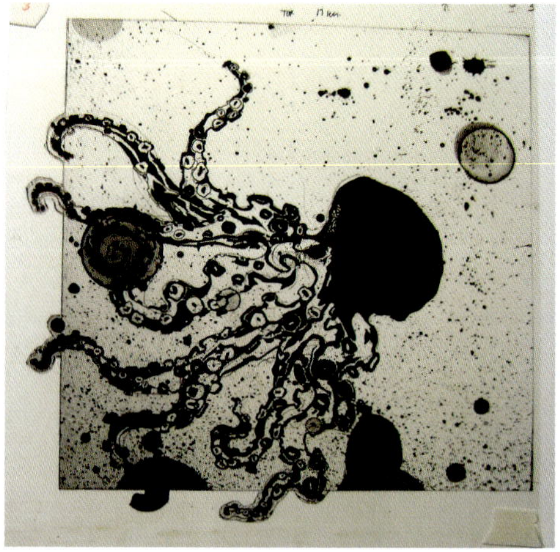

3

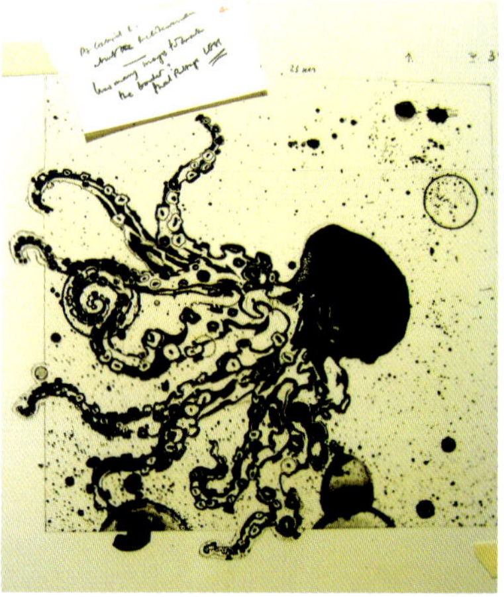

4

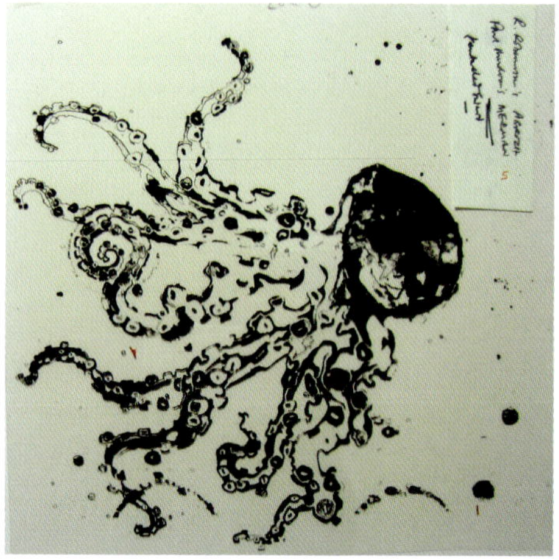

5

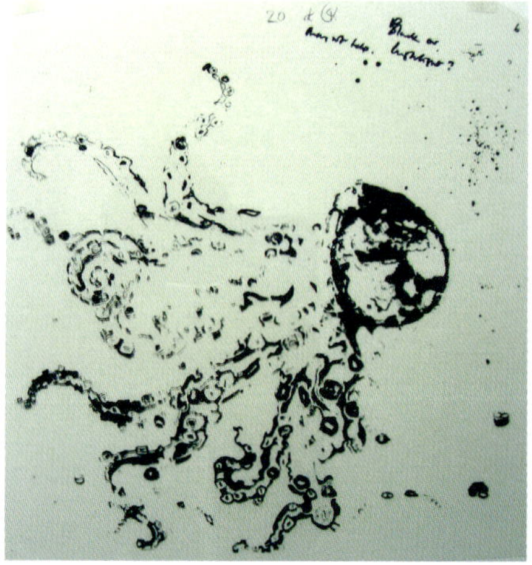

6

3, *4*, *5* and *6* were used in *Primrose And Ultramarine* (p. 41) after extensive reworking of separations and on the screens in four dilutions of the French Ultramarine. The print-process necessitates a Janus-like approach, one constantly thinks forwards and backwards as each new layer covers elements of those preceding it. The degree of translucency or opacity of the colours will reveal or block out the previous layers.

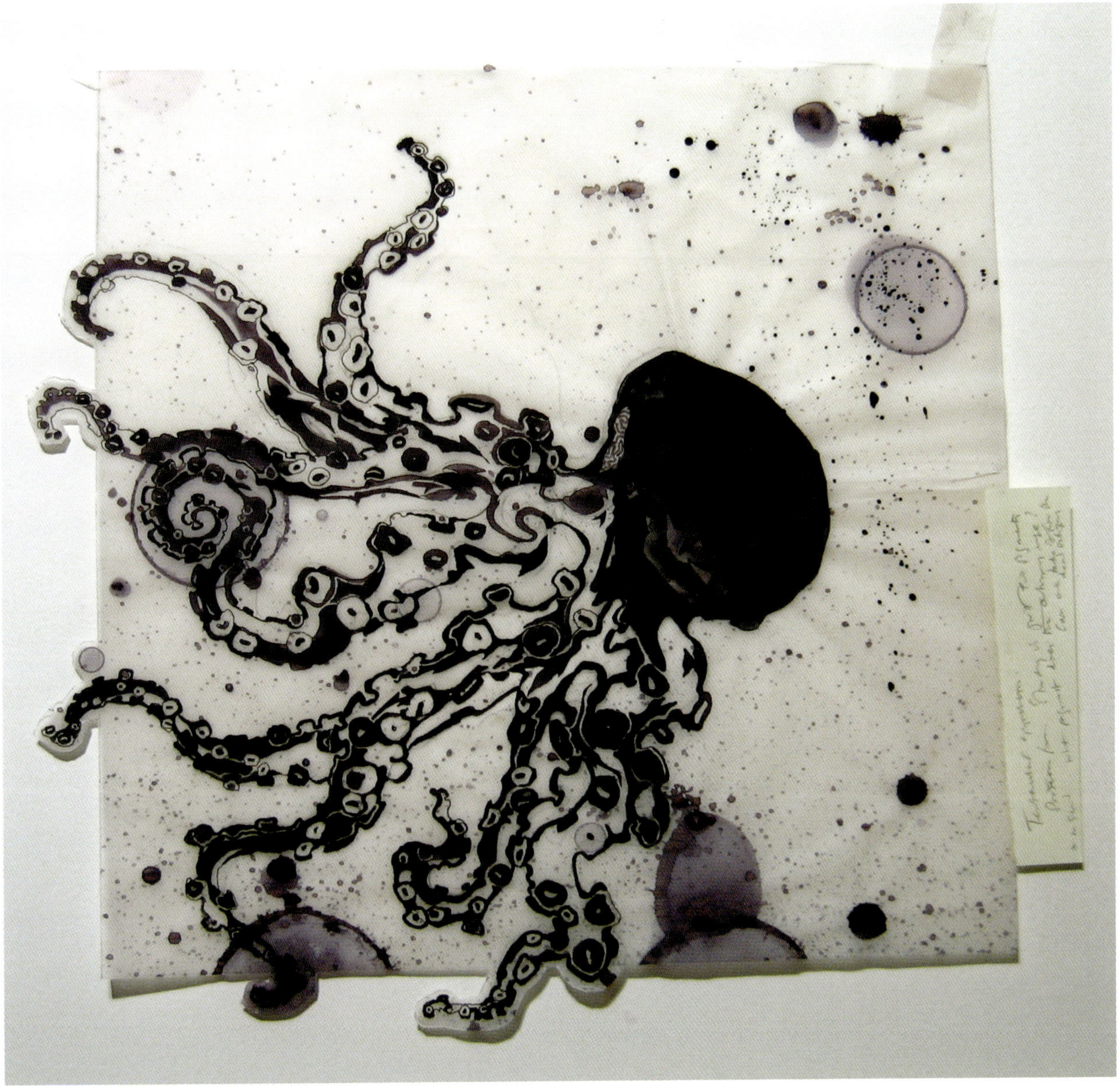

Ink drawing on transparent paper (see p. 41)

Alcuni di noi giocavano a pallavolo, alcuni
bevevano da Perroni, altri andavono all'interno
cercando selci e sorgenti di acqua chiara.

Io vagavo sulla riva verso il porto
sotto il faro di Palinuro
e trovai un delfino rotolato dalla marea

gravamente
pesantamente, la pelle scorticata sui ciottoli aguzzi;
poi, magra, leale, la voce del timoniere
tornò delle ombre e una luce colpì

attraverso il tuonare muto della roccia
a Cumae, mentre la pazza, per calmarlo, disse
«Quel luogo per sempre porterà il tuo nome»

Jamie McKendrick, initial scripting of *Margin* in Italian (p. 25)

Notes on 'Margin'

This poem was written in Oxford, early in January 1990, not long after returning from Salerno where I'd been living for four years. Its setting is a small coastal town to the south of Salerno, Palinuro, named after Aeneas's helmsman of whom it was forecast he would lie shroudless on an unknown strand: "nudus in ignota, Palinure, iacebis harena", in the last line of Book V, The Aeniad. A passage from the visit to the underworld in Book VI (l.642-) must have given me my opening – in W.F. Jackson Knight's prose translation:

> Of these bright spirits, some were taking exercise at games together on the grass of a field of play, or wrestling on yellow sand. Others were treading a rhythmic dance and as they danced they sang…

(there's a reworking of this in Paradise Lost Bk. II, l.528-581: "Part on the plain, or in the air sublime/ Upon the wing, or in swift race contended…Others more mild/ Retreated in a silent valley, sing…").

For the ending I've also borrowed from Aeniad Bk. VI where Palinurus recounts how he was murdered by Italian tribesmen (l.340-), and later where the Sybil of Cumae consoles him by telling of his tomb: "that place shall bear the name of Palinurus for ever".

The poem belongs to a sequence of nine poems called 'Lost Cities', set in specific – and imaginary – sites around the Mediterranean, and in which there are also other references to Aeneas's voyages. All this sounds very literary, full of classical bric-a-brac, but much of the detail of this poem comes from frequent visits, innocent of any scholarly intent, to a beach near Palinuro. And I guess the presence of so much remaining Greek and Roman architecture in this region has the effect of making the classics seem almost contemporary.

As for the drafts, the first I have is in Italian. I'm not sure why I should have attempted something so unnatural. It's possibly a translation from a still earlier version in English, just to try out how it sounded, though it may even have been my first attempt. The next, dated one is in English, very close, though eliminating the "us" of the first line ("Alcuni di noi"- some of us) and already settling on "the stringy, knifed wheeze of the helmsman". The next and last draft is almost final – only "the rooted chambers of the rock" is still unresolved. This finally turns into "the mute larynx of the rock" which includes elements of the earlier "mute thunder" and "rooted chamber" and has something of the look of the actual keyhole- shaped tunnel at Cumae. All three versions manage to misspell the name of the Italian beer.

Notes on *Margin*, excerpt from letter by Jamie McKendrick

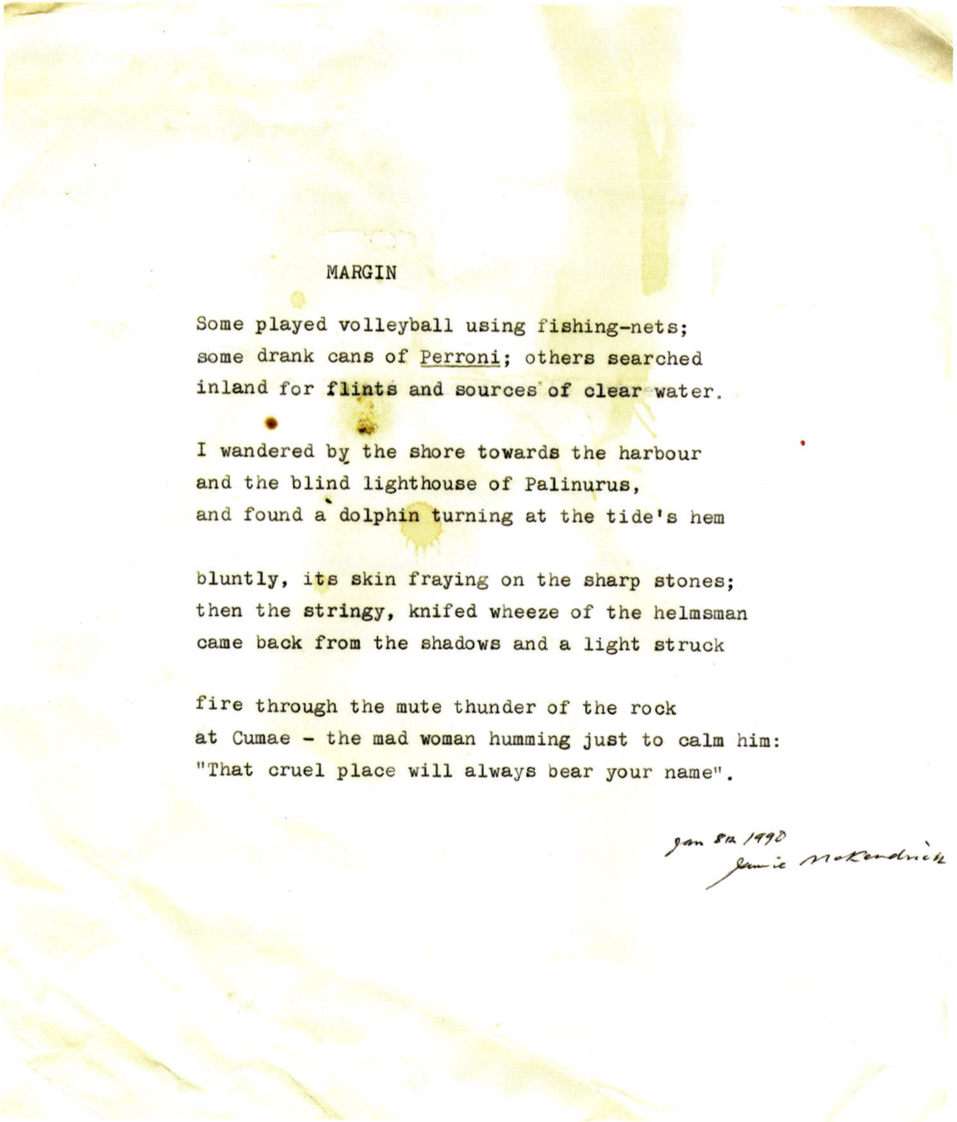

MARGIN

Some played volleyball using fishing-nets;
some drank cans of Perroni; others searched
inland for flints and sources of clear water.

I wandered by the shore towards the harbour
and the blind lighthouse of Palinurus,
and found a dolphin turning at the tide's hem

bluntly, its skin fraying on the sharp stones;
then the stringy, knifed wheeze of the helmsman
came back from the shadows and a light struck

fire through the mute thunder of the rock
at Cumae - the mad woman humming just to calm him:
"That cruel place will always bear your name".

Jan 8th 1998
Jamie McKendrick

Jamie McKendrick, *Margin*, typed version (p. 25)

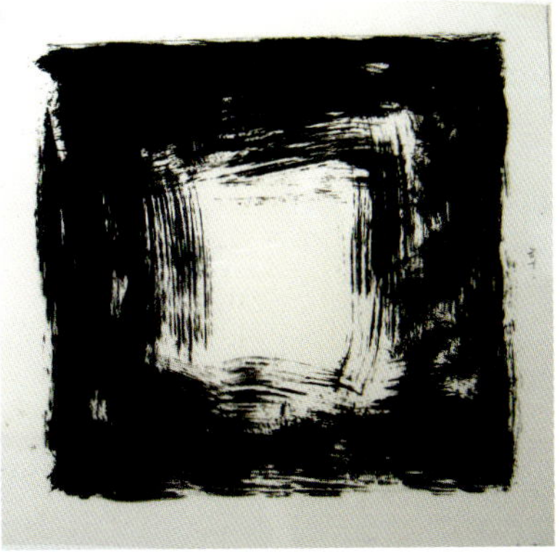

1

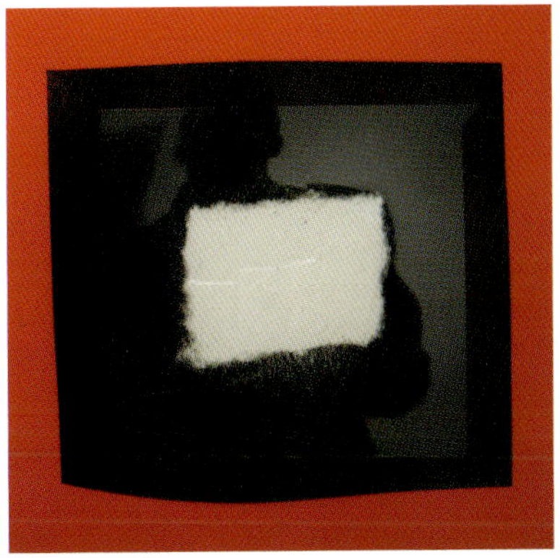

2

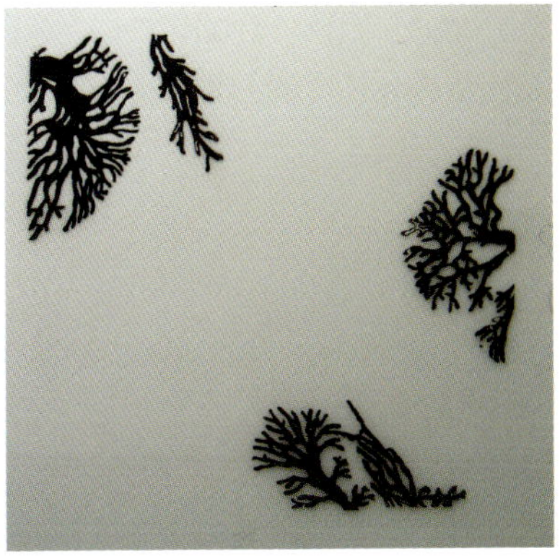

3

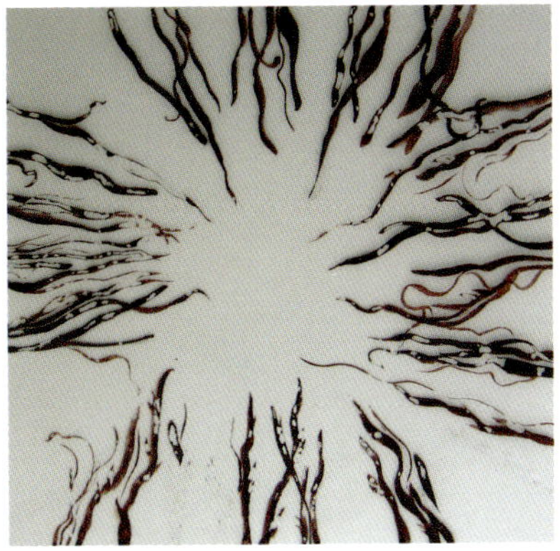

4

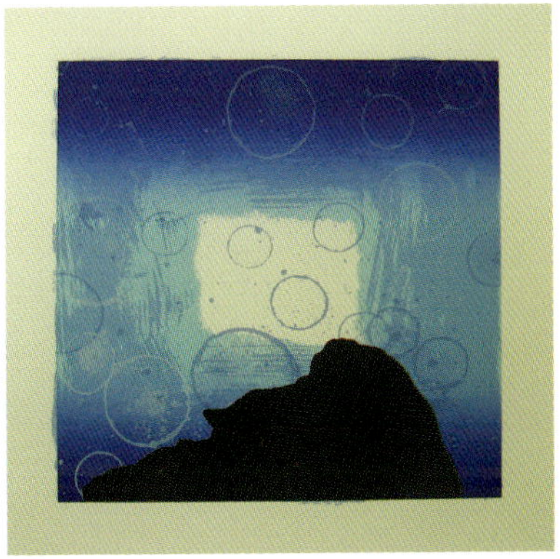

5

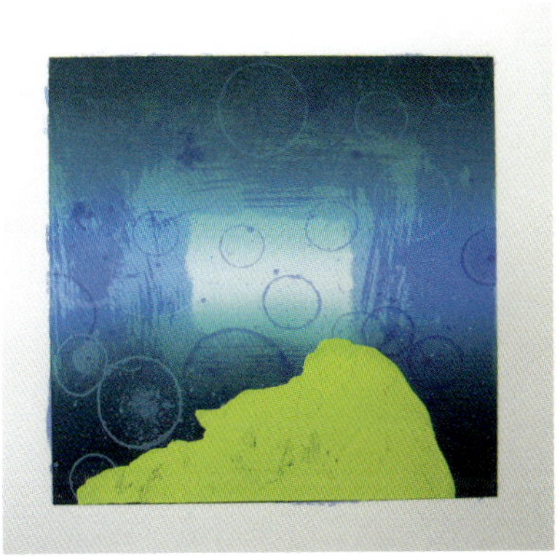

6

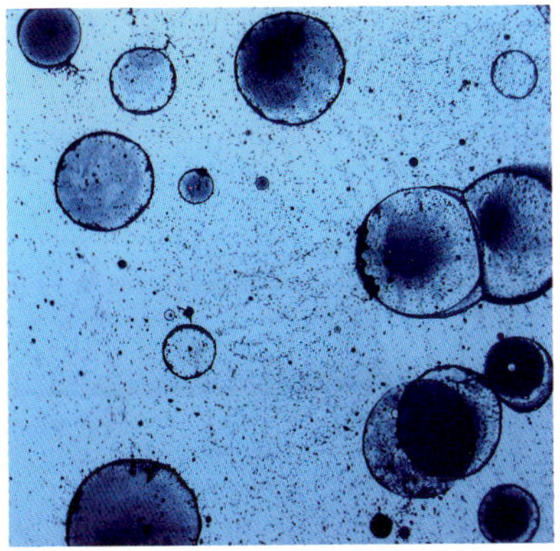

7

1. Brushstrokes: first printing in Monastral blue plus Monastral green
2. Pale Monastral blue
3. Black coral forms
4. Mid-tone Monastral blue centering
5. Showing blend, top and base (colour proof rejected) plus rock form
6. Rejected proof
7. Rejected proof
8. *Coming Up For Air*, final version (see p. 31)

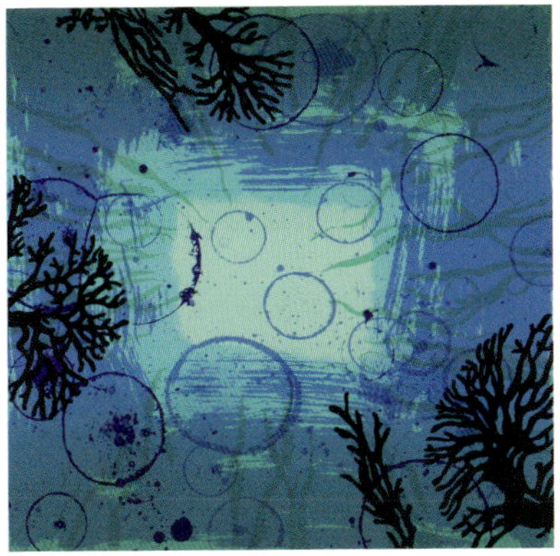

8

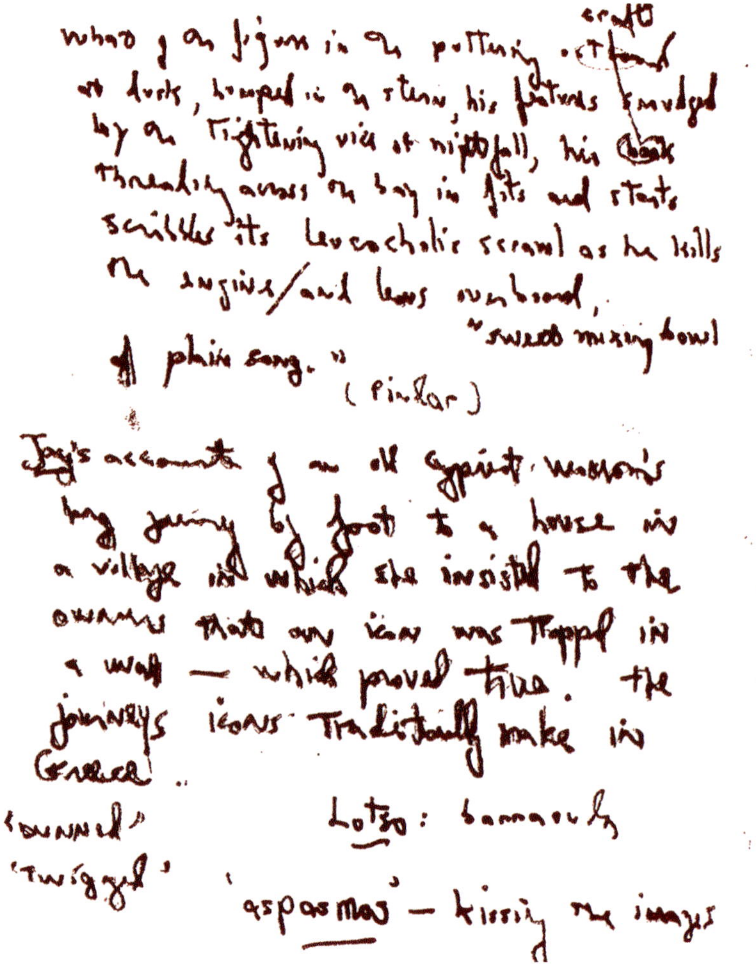

whose figure in the pottering craft/boat
at dusk, hunched in the stern, his features smudged
by the tightening vise of nightfall, his [illegible]
threading across the bay in fits and starts
scribbles its leucocholic scrawl as he kills
the engine/and leans overboard,
"sweet mixing bowl
of plain song." (Pindar)

Joy's account of an old Cypriot woman's
long journey by foot to a house in
a village in which she insisted to the
owners that an icon was trapped in
a wall — which proved true. the
journeys icons traditionally make in
Greece.

'sunned' Lotso: bannarly
'twigged'
'aspasmos' — kissing the images

Gabriel Levin, field notebook from Cyprus (notes retraced by the poet after it was dampened)

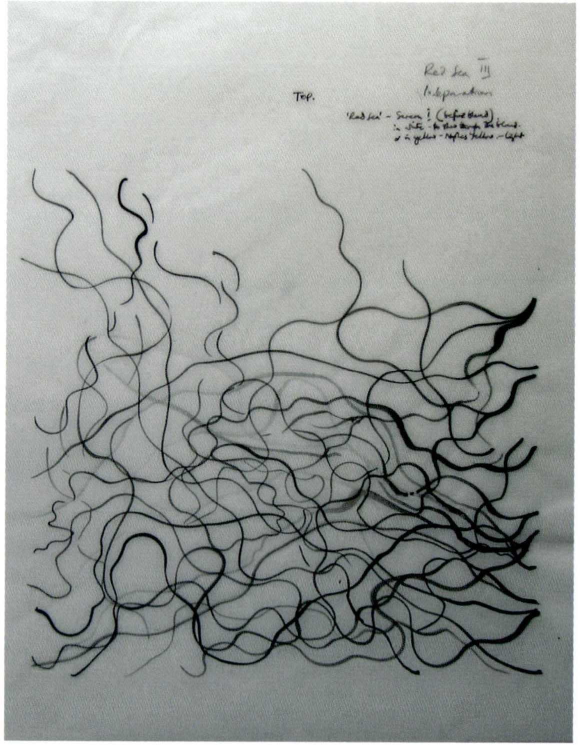

Image used in: *Gulf* (pp. 9 and 11), first printing in lemon yellow); *Medusa* (pp. 14 and 49), final printing in milky-white); *Underwavebreak* (pp. 39 and 103), last two screens, printed in cream-white and pale Cerulean blue.

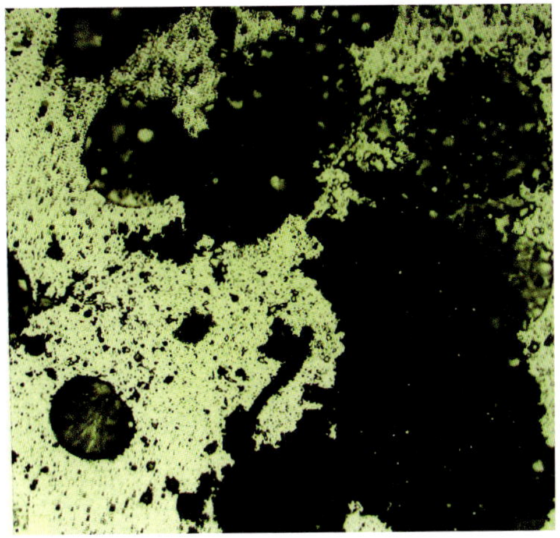

Bubble-form (left): see *Red Sea* (p. 27) and *Proteus* (p. 37).

Images *2* and *3* were used in *Red Sea*. This was one of the few instances where the colour of the drawing matched that of the printed ink. Generally one draws or paints in black and must imagine the effect of the line or mark as it will later 'read' in the colours of the print.

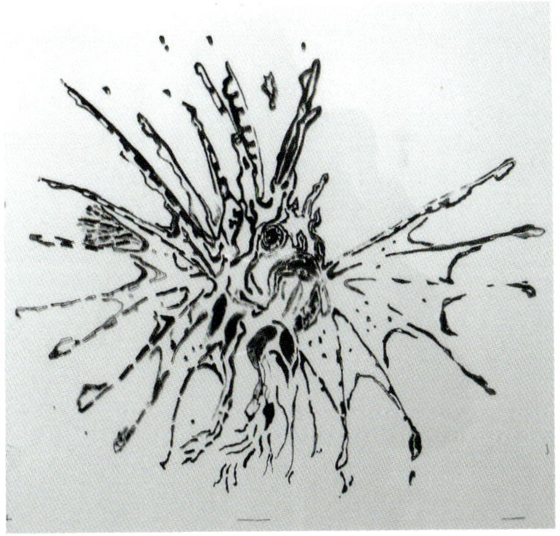

1

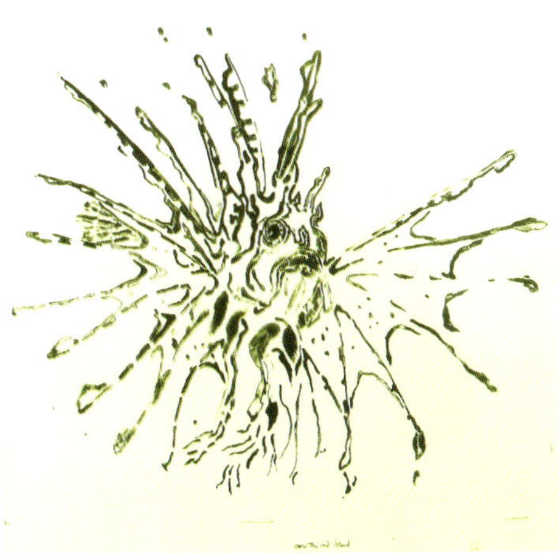

2

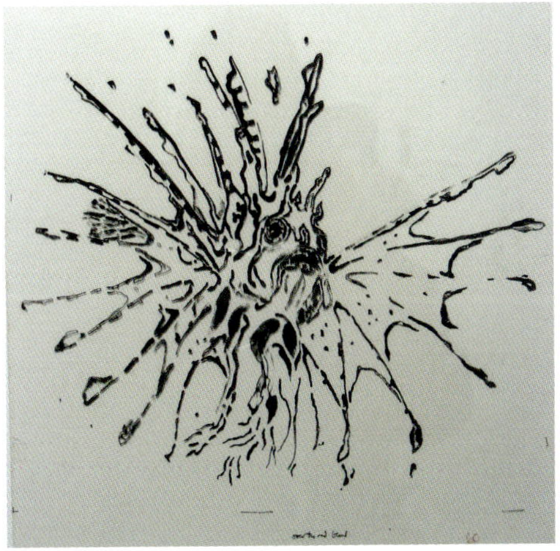

3

les ruines de Dora

Tantura lagoon/ Tel Dor

Mediterranean

murex shells — the royal dye being squeezed
out of the hypobranchial gland — Litter
the shore, where Sea People once hauled
long ships into the eastern basin, seeking her
who'd given them the slip — Beauty
they hallowed in her wake, or some such name
barked from the belly at the cross mutiny.
In their polychrome robes they stood in vain
gaping at the sea, the surf's short-
breathed plosives detonating in their ears.
Now I skim the busy beach for sport,
Lady-of-the-Sea, forever in arrears
of love, ears cocked to the pulmonary beat
of young hearts primed by the heat.

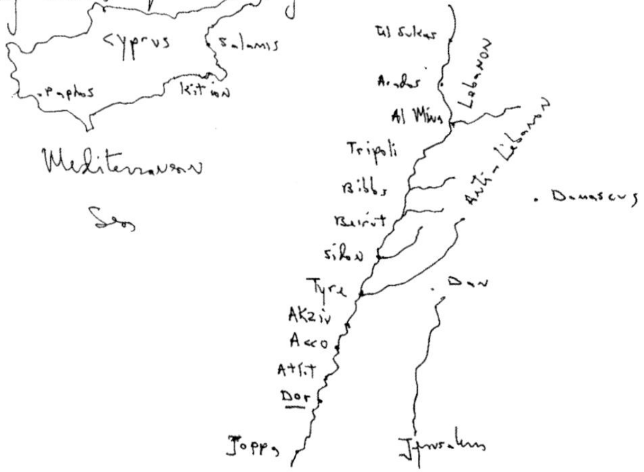

Gabriel Levin, scripting of *Mediterranean* (see p. 16)

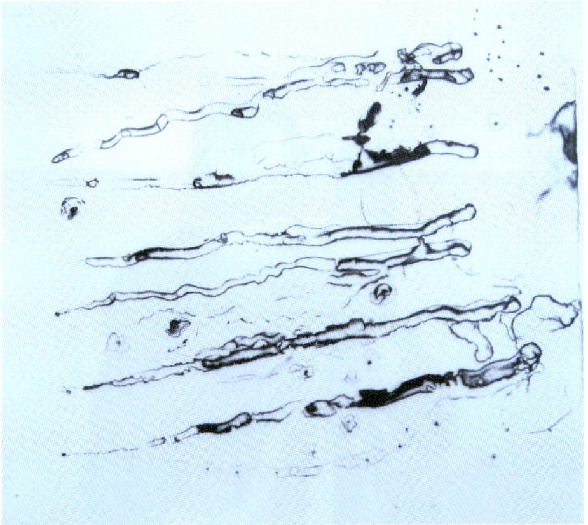

1

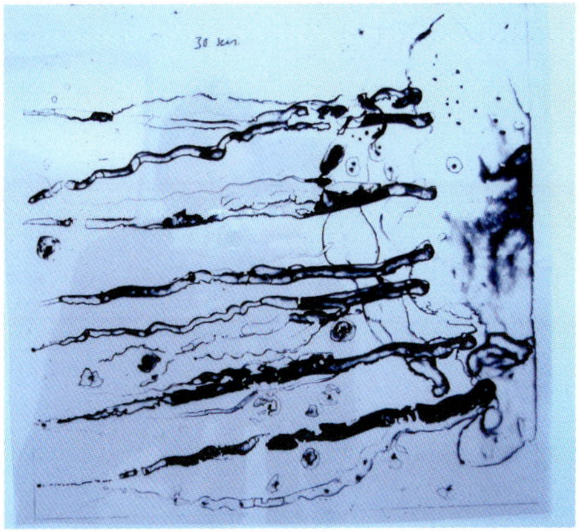

2

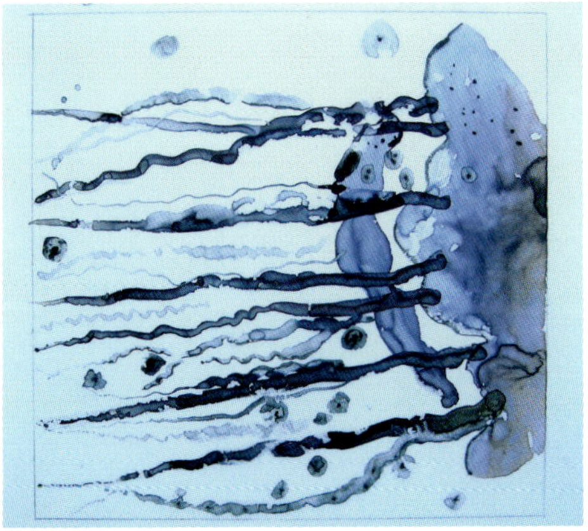

3

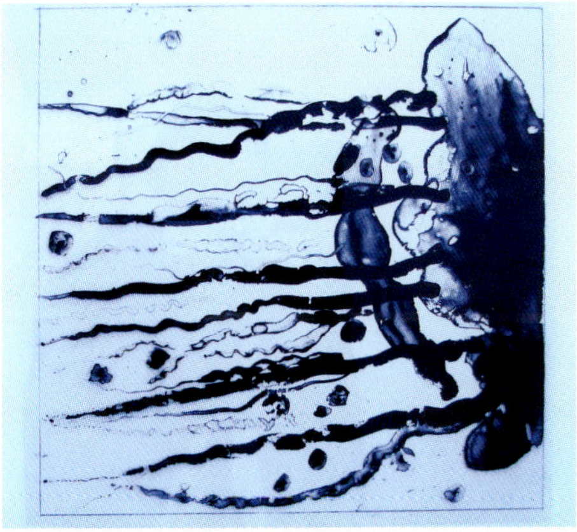

4

These were the 3rd, 4th, 5th and 6th printings of *Medusa* (p. 14).

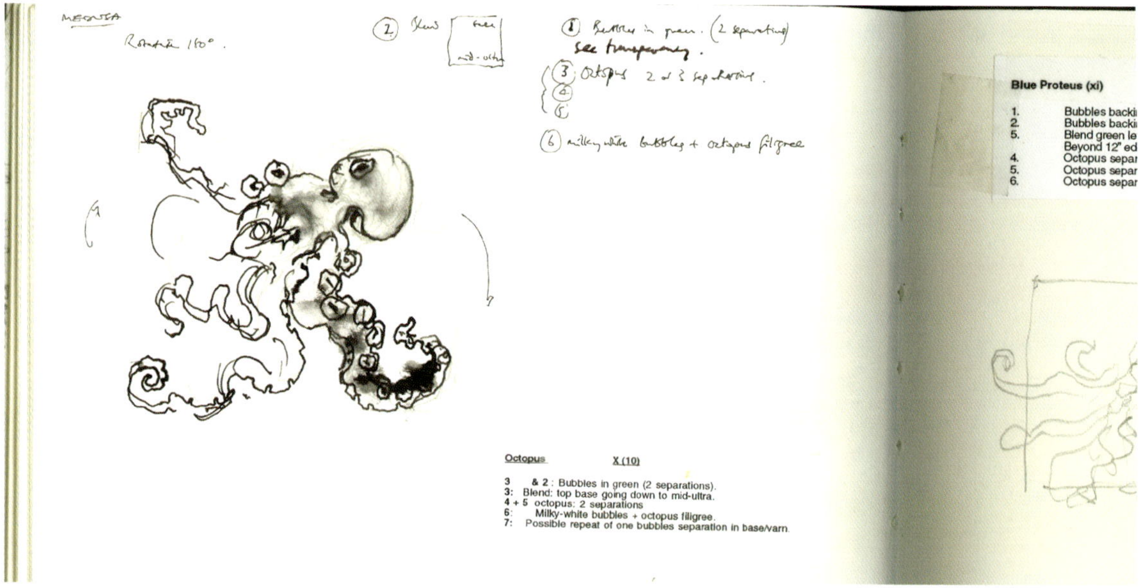

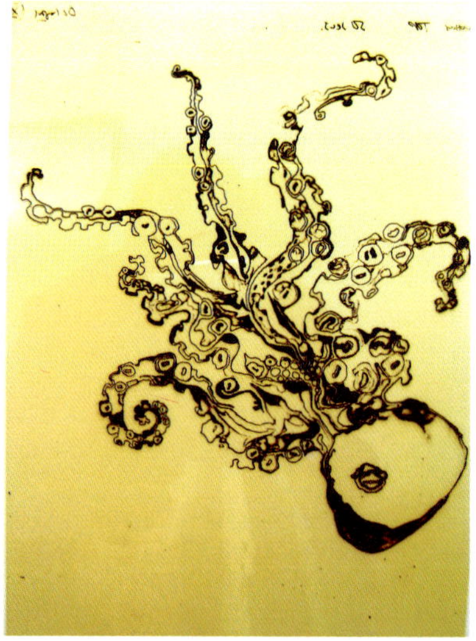

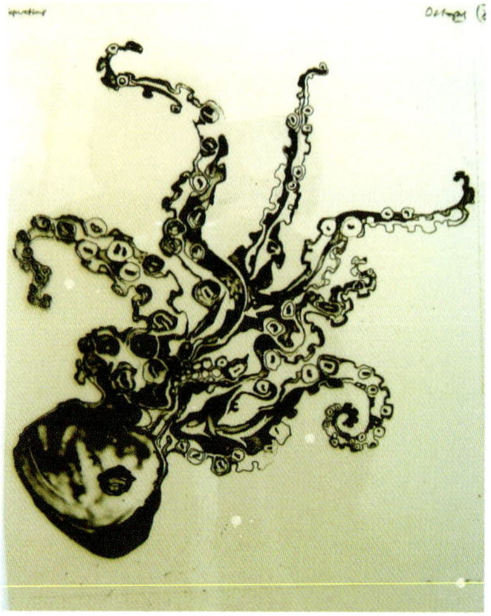

Sketches for *Proteus* (p. 37)

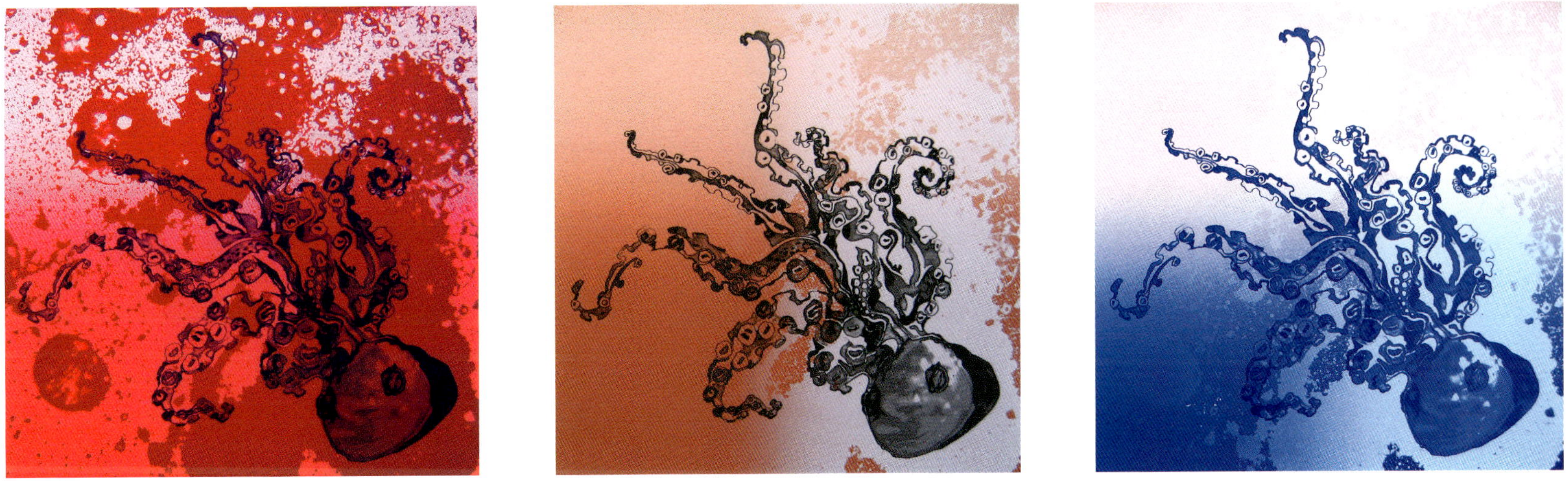

Proteus: proofs towards the final image

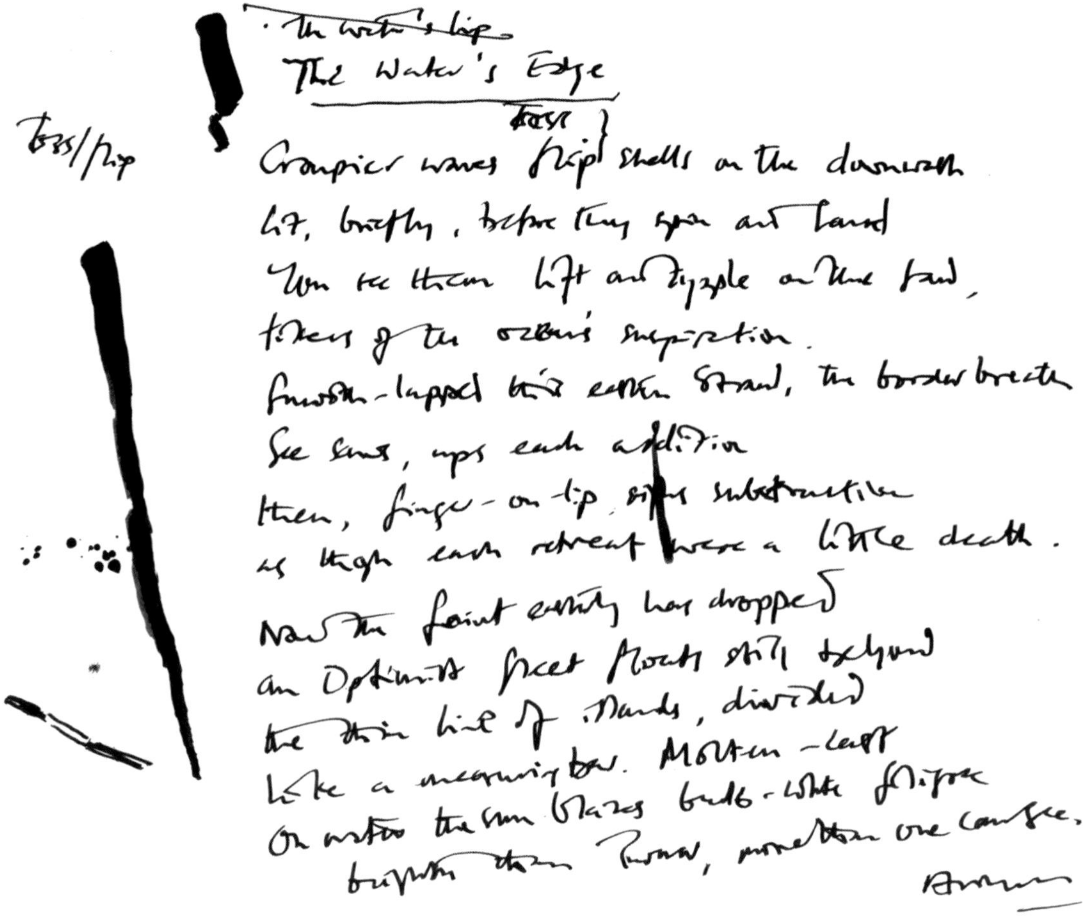

Detail of **Octopot**: ceramic engraving by Ardyn Halter on pot turned by Asnat Halter

Ardyn Halter, *The Water's Edge* (p. 46)

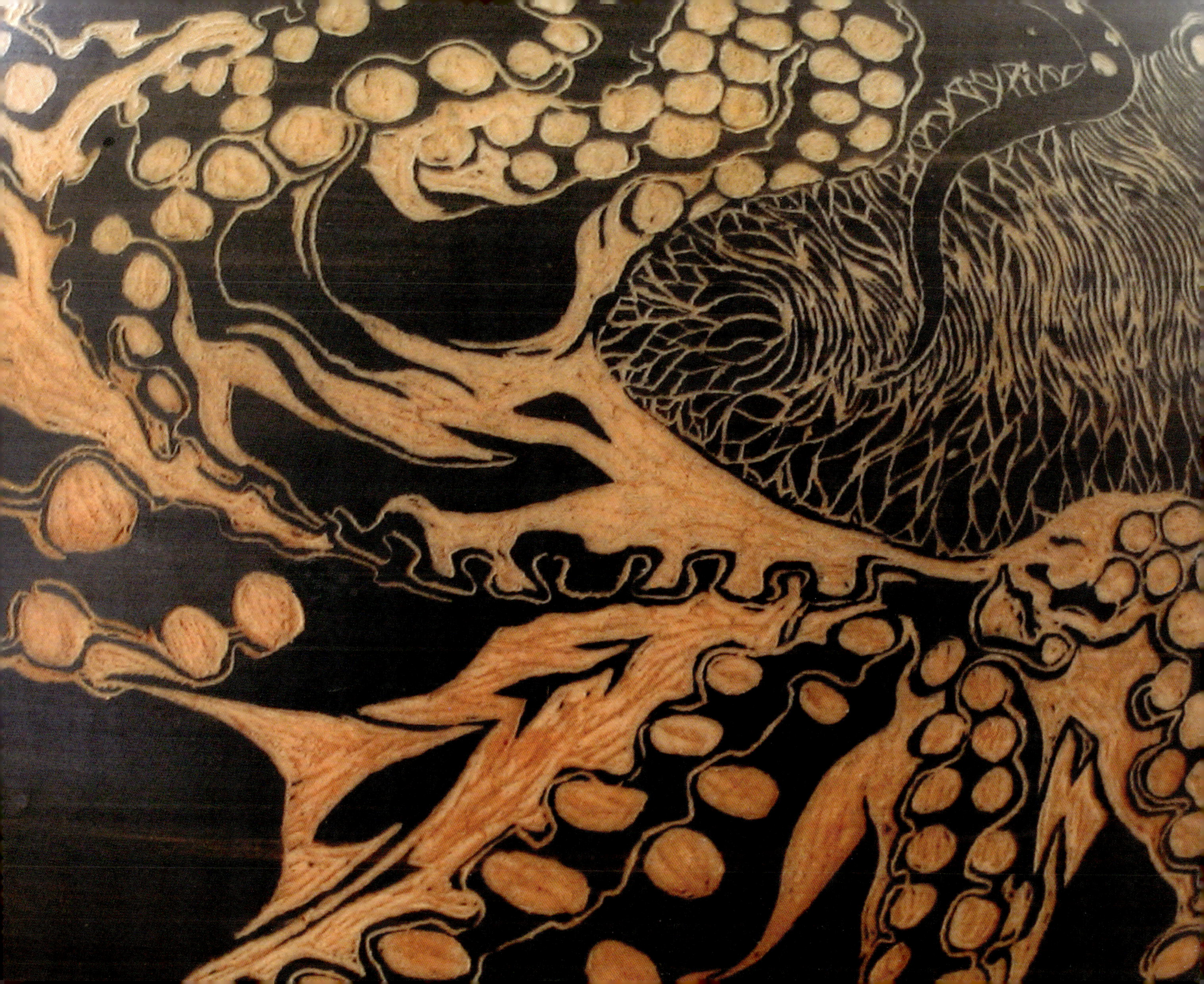

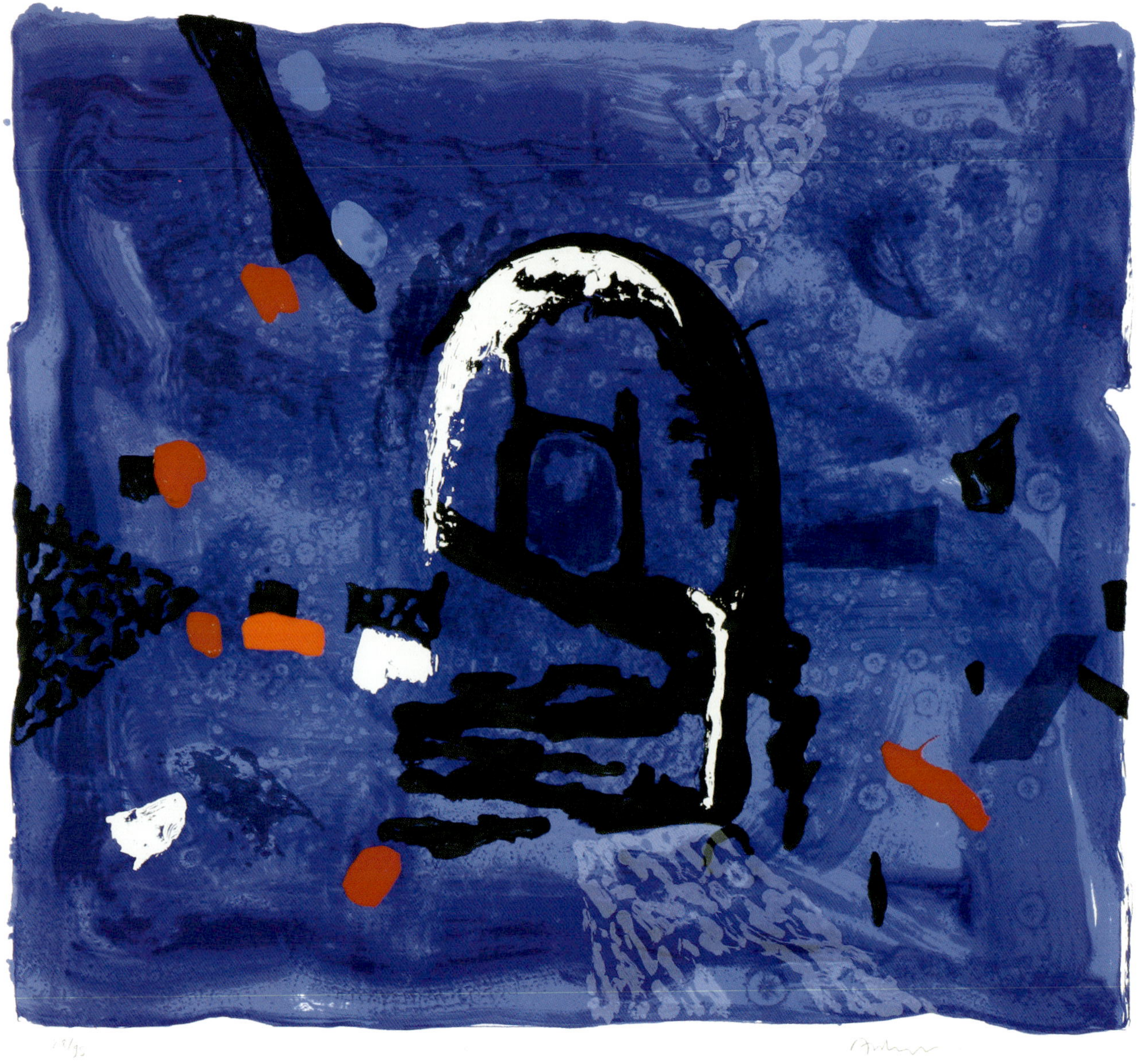

Streets of the River, 13-colour silkscreen plus 8 woodblocks, 2000 (edition of 95). Size: 88 × 102 cm; 35 × 40 in

The Taninim Stream, Amiqam

to Ariel Halperin on his fiftieth birthday

The black arthritic vines twist, slough off their bark.
The leaden heart, the leaden casing surprised,
the bud's discharge, unshapen showing
a glistening pigment extruded stark
from the tube, yellow-green, from old stock, surprised
at its own unfolding. Wings strengthening
in light. They know neither hamsin
fifty days from now, nor even night –
untested as a thought before it's aired.
Hesitate before a feather breeze
wafts aniseed or mustard. Commotion
of sap, fricative grass. Not a step certain
as the chill March stream cuts its simple flow
about your ankles, makes the least of you.

Ardyn Halter

When printmaking, I find it more stimulating to come to the print workshop with images that I have verbalized rather than sketched out. This reticence, avoidance of clarified preset images is intentional. I don't want to restrict myself to preconceived images that would shackle the process of printmaking but instead prefer to allow the tangents, the chance occurrences, luck or sortilege of the screen to pull me in new directions.

So more often than not I list ideas. It is somehow easier to stray from a list of words than from premeditated images. Some images, as they appeared, shifted and found themselves in other prints. Indeed, most images have at least one screen in common.

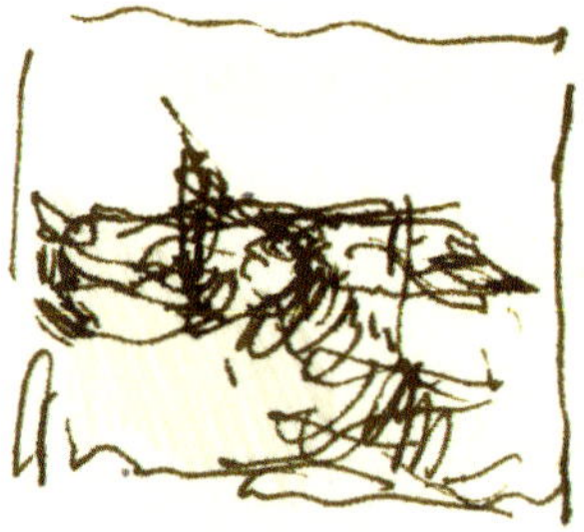

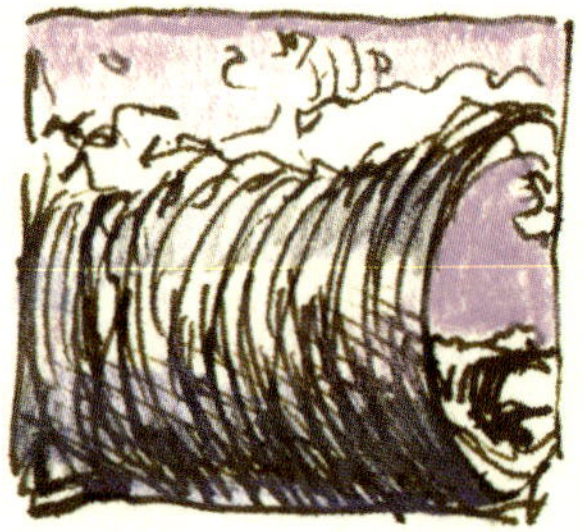

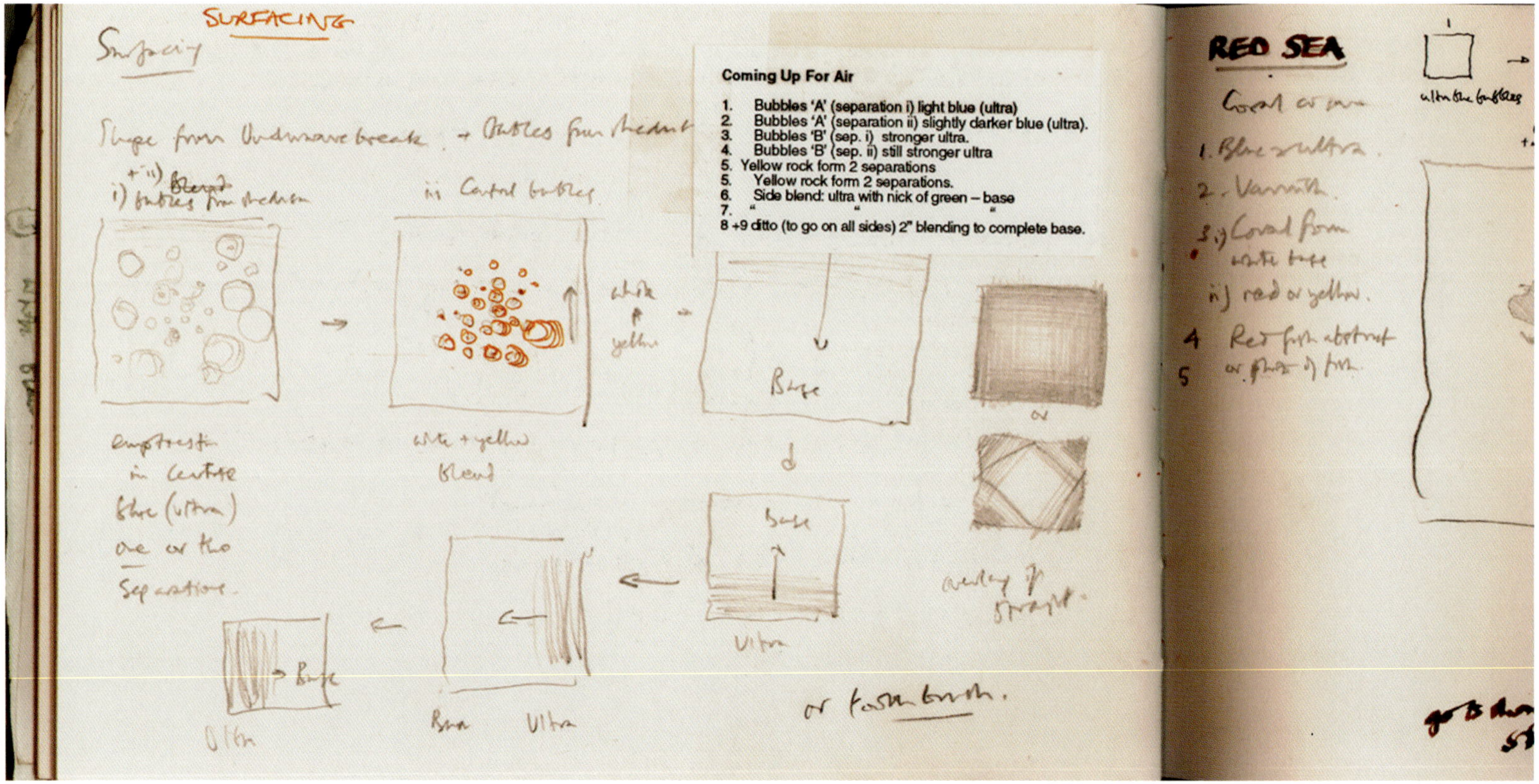

Pibroch

Foam in the sand-lap of the north-sea water
fizzles out — leaves the beach mouthing —
the flecks of the last kiss
kissed away by the next wave, rushing;
each shearing over its own sea-valve
as it turns with a shock into sound.

And how I long now for the pibroch,
pibroch long and slow, lamenting all this:
all this longing for the right wave,
for the special wave that toils
behind the pilot but can never find a home —
find my edge to crash against,
my darkness for its darknesses
my hands amongst its foam.

Robin Robertson, *Pibroch* (overleaf)

Pibroch

Foam in the sand-lap of the north-sea water
fizzles out – leaves the beach mouthing –
the flecks of the last kiss
kissed away by the next wave, rushing;
each shearing over its own sea-valve
as it turns with a shock into sound.

And how I long now for the pibroch,
pibroch long and slow, lamenting all this:
all this longing for the right wave,
for the special wave that toils
behind the pilot but can never find a home –
find my edge to crash against,
my darkness for its darknesses
my hands amongst its foam.

Robin Robertson

From *A Painted Field*, Picador, 1997

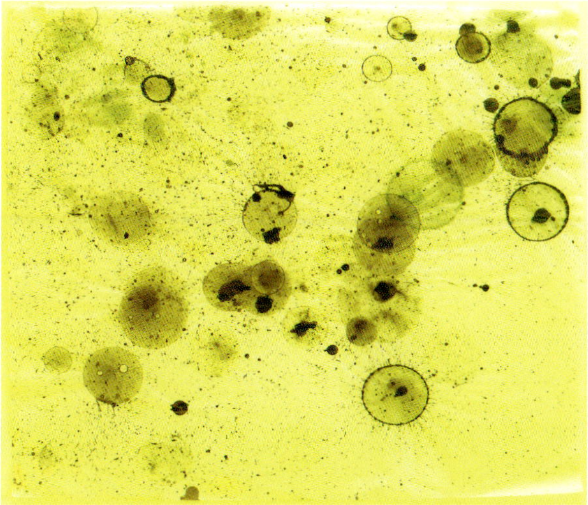

1

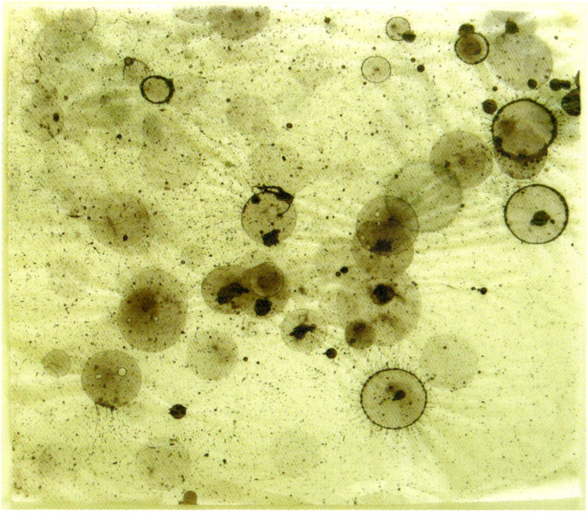

2

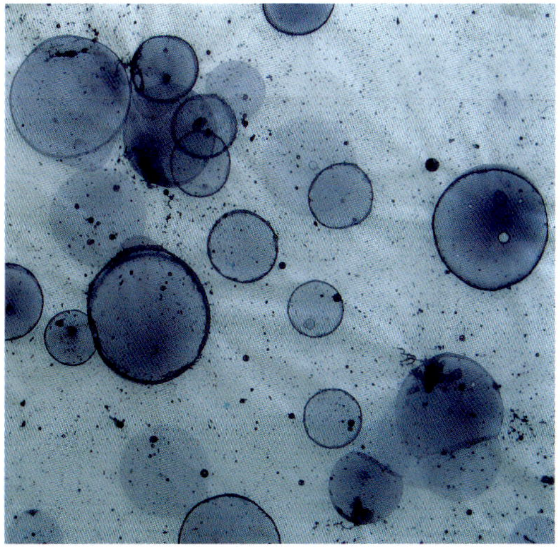

3

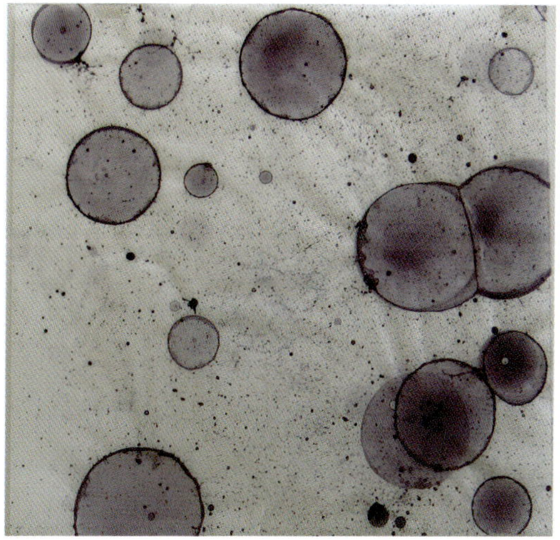

4

Bubbles: *1* and *2* were used during proofings but later abandoned; *3* and *4* were integrated in *Coming Up For Air* (p. 31).

died of bad luck

A Fifth String

Scuttling crabwise all ~~knees~~ elbows and ~~elbows~~ knees
– {a dancer's inspired deformity?}–
she ~~gives a cheery wave~~ waves a wild hello with outsize
pincers and ~~is gone, a black-suited~~ a ~~slick haired~~ man in grinning close-up
thrums ~~strums~~ ~~is playing something lively on~~ a hairbrush banjo-style
(banjo-style..) ~~But the spectacle falters~~ even though it's over
and I'm ~~into~~ waking

to a ship's ~~long call~~ colossal blare across the bay–
stunning ~~a single note that stuns~~ the air, humming
~~its certainty humming~~ in the bones with ~~certainty~~
like ~~as~~ a tuning fork struck ~~single note~~ into song.
Behind closed lids I hear it fathoms down,
that sunken A ~~so~~ a bass ~~ear~~ night reach ~~without~~
on some ~~a strange~~ fifth string.

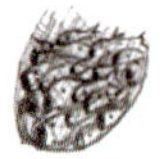

Dennis Potter
synchronicities

sfumato

And I wish the sea had kept to itself
the evening catch hauled up through livid silk.
All those sardine eyes seeing everything and
nothing for the first time. Perfect mouths
open, shut, losing the beat, miming
deadpan a music-hall number, its tender
absurdities

James Wright – "Its ecstasy is dead"
poetics of the irretrievable

absurd ditties

Jennie Feldman, draft of *A Fifth String*

Odysseus

And lustrous Calypso quickly led the way . . .

Sometimes I could swear it's the other
voice murmuring long-distance in my ear.
But the shape you take in the dark
is yours, these hands having long since lost
all memory of home . . . Then the crunch
come morning and shells' dead glory
underfoot. Immortality? But I'm dying
of this protracted present tense, the sea's
unbearable sameness without me.
These nights that hang an anchor-stone
smooth around my neck – till I'm thrashing
for air, clinging fast, washed up sprawling
in the surf, again, as the static hiss
all but drowns Odysseus, Odysseus . . .

Jennie Feldman

From *The Lost Notebook*, Anvil, 2005

Shhh

Then, it was natural
to hear the sea remembered
in those stony arches and chambers
though I soon knew it might as well
be anything – forest fires, landslides, hurricanes
falsified by distance
or amplification; the white noise
of the wilder elements

or the wild chaos
as she puts her lips to your ear
and you cock your brain to catch
the general drift – the blandishments,
the breath drawn at your touch:
I no longer believe what I hear.

Don Paterson, *Shhh* (p. 27)

What Seas What Shores
1998
edition: 75
15-colour silkscreen
plus 3 woodblocks
120 × 130 cm; 51 × 54 in

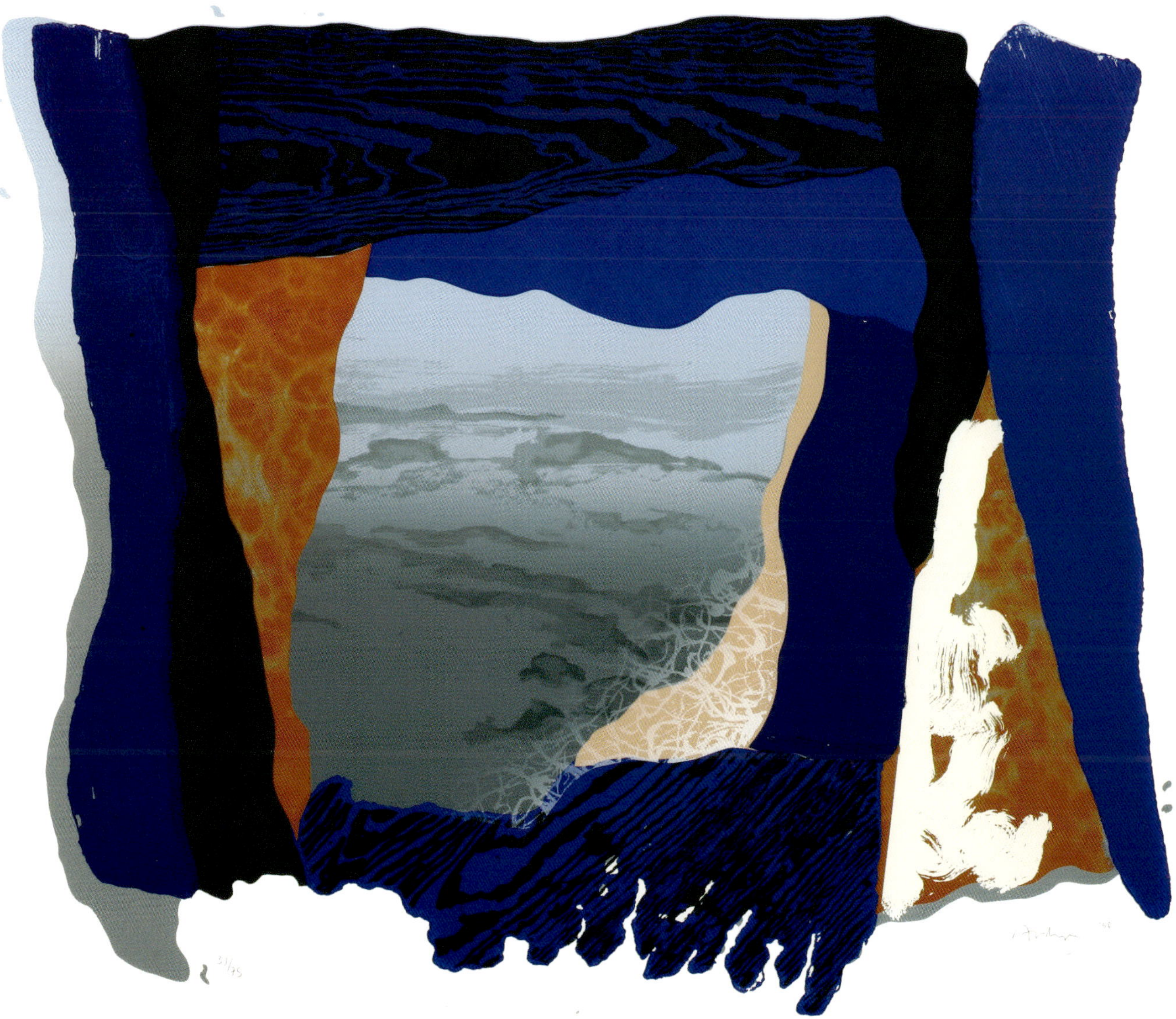

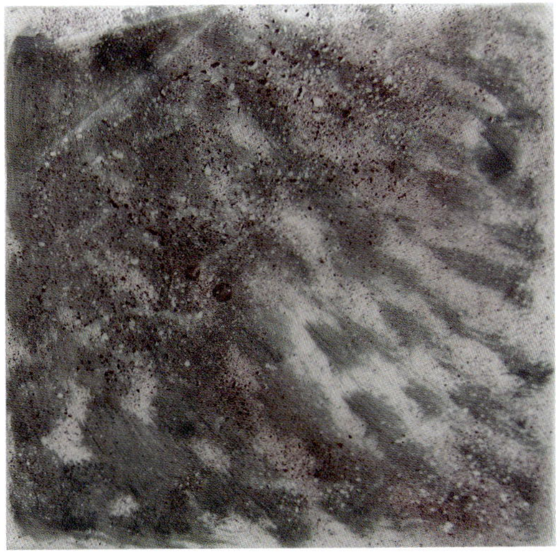

1

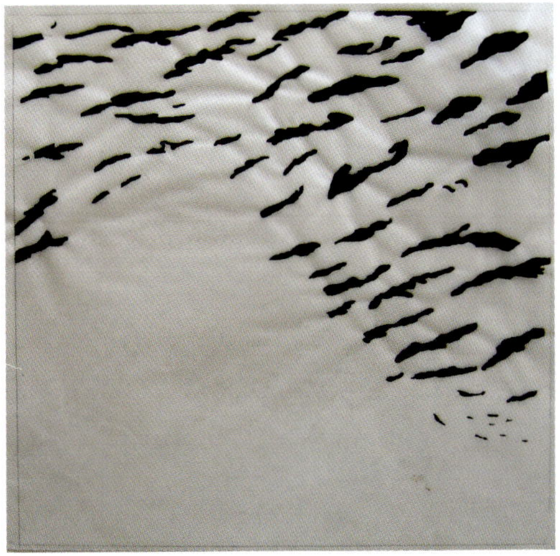

2

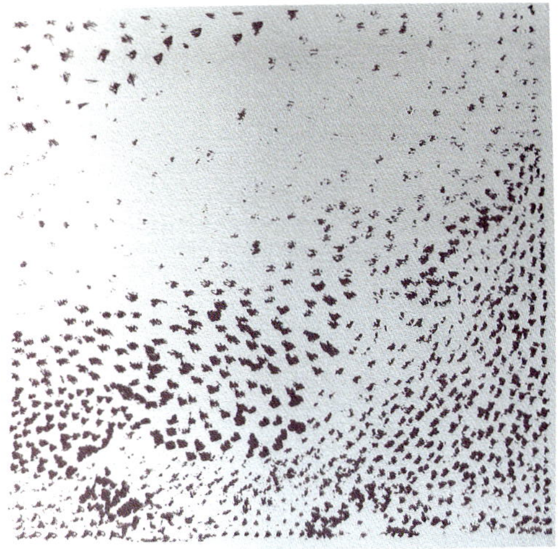

3

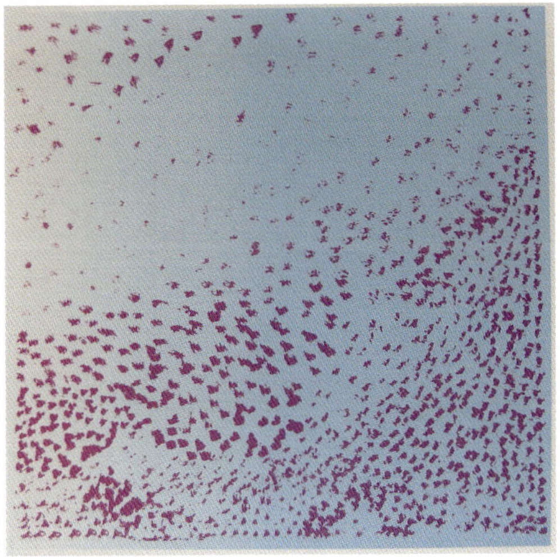

4

Sargasso
detail
(p. 31)

1. Prepared but not used in *Underwavebreak*. *2*. Watersurface: Ultramarine-base in *Are Coral Made* (p. 17). *3* and *4* were intended for a print that was never realised.

Underwavebreak
detail
(p. 39)

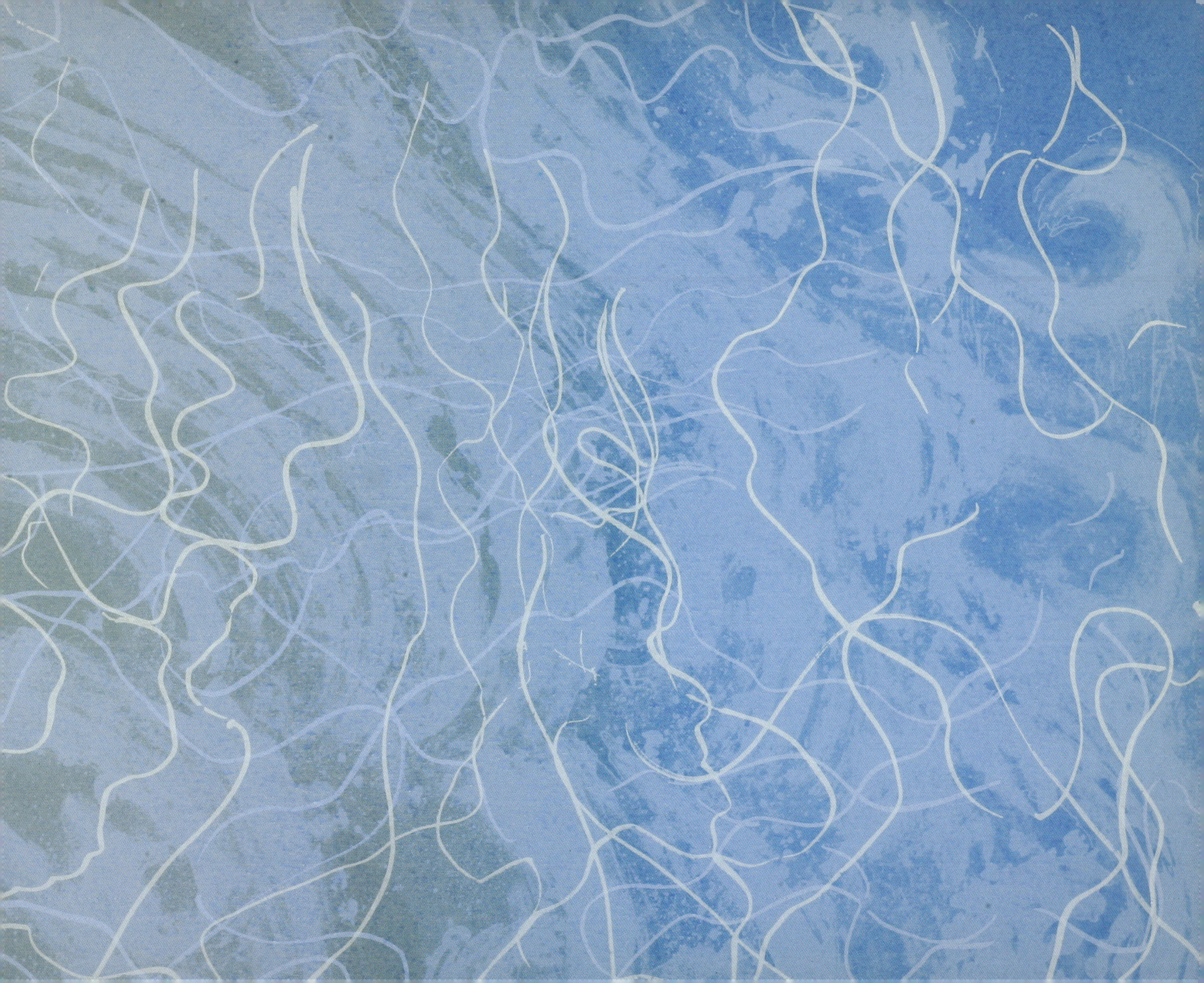

Acknowledgements

Particular thanks to Seamus Heaney, Geoffrey Hill, Michael Longley, Jamie McKendrick, Paul Muldoon, Don Paterson, Robin Robertson and to Stephen Romer, Jennie Feldman and Gabriel Levin for their encouragement.

Thanks to Robert Saich and the team at Advanced Graphics, to Cameron Lindo and to Scott Campbell; to Rob Handrill of Bookworks.

Thanks to Haya Bernstein for her genial patience when we worked on the design; to Ran Erde for the photography.

Thanks to Russell Parton and Sally Jeffery and all involved at Lund Humphries, and in particular to my publisher Nigel Farrow for his faith in a book that resists categories.

Thanks to Dr Jeremiah Losty, Dr Christopher Fletcher and Dr Richard Price of The British Library; to Richard Selby and Richard Gault, The Redfern Gallery; to my friend Horace Richter for his eye and his encouragement over the years; to Leonard Milberg; to Roberta Wadell, The New York Public Library; to H.E. Sherard Cowper-Coles, Her Majesty's Ambassador to Saudi Arabia; to Peter Noser; to Jean Marks; to Sue Jupp; to Ellen Fischl-Bodner; to my sister Aloma Halter; to my parents Roman and Susie Halter.